The Person and Work of the Holy Spirit

J. C. Ryle

Monergism Books

Published by by Monergism Books
P.O. Box 491
West Linn Oregon 97068
www.monergism.com

ISBN: 978-1-961807-70-9

Contents

Chapter One

The Holy Spirit

"If anyone does not have the Spirit of Christ, he does not belong to Him." (Romans 8:9)

The subject of this paper is one of the deepest importance to our souls. That subject is the work of God the Holy Spirit. The solemn words of the text which heads this page demand the attention of all who believe the Scriptures to be the living voice of God. "If anyone does not have the Spirit of Christ, he does not belong to Him."

It is probable that most of those into whose hands this paper will fall, have been baptized. And in what name were you baptized? It was "in the name of the Father, and of the Son, and of the Holy Spirit."

It is probable that many readers of this paper are married people. And in what name were you pronounced man and wife together? Again, it was "in the name of the Father, and of the Son, and of the Holy Spirit."

It is not unlikely that many readers of this paper are members of the Church of England. And in what do you declare your belief every Sunday, when you repeat the Creed? You say that you "believe in God the Father, and in God the Son, and in God the Holy Spirit."

It is likely that many readers of this paper will be buried one day with
the burial service of the Church of England. And what will be the last
words pronounced over your coffin, before the mourners go home, and
the grave closes over your head? They will be, "may the grace of our Lord
Jesus Christ, and the love of God, and the fellowship of the Holy Spirit
be with you all." (2 Cor. 13:14.)

Now I ask every reader of this paper a plain question Do you know
what you mean by these words, so often repeated—the Holy Spirit?
What place has God the Holy Spirit in your religion? What do you know
of His office, His work, His indwelling, His fellowship, and His power?
This is the subject to which I ask your attention this day. I want you
to consider seriously what you know about the work of God the Holy
Spirit.

I believe that the times in which we live demand frequent and distinct
testimonies upon this great subject. I believe that few truths of the
Christian religion are so often obscured and spoiled by false doctrine as
the truth about the Holy Spirit. I believe that there is no subject which an
ignorant world is so ready to revile as "cant, fanaticism, and enthusiasm,"
as the subject of the work of the Holy Spirit. My heart's desire and prayer
to God is, that about this subject I may write nothing but the "truth as it
is in Jesus," and that I may write that truth in love. For convenience sake
I shall divide my subject into four heads. I shall examine in order—

I. Firstly—the **importance** attached to the work of the Holy Spirit in
Scripture.

II. Secondly—the **necessity** of the work of the Holy Spirit to man's
salvation.

III. Thirdly—the **manner** in which the Holy Spirit works in man's
heart.

IV. Lastly—the **marks** and **evidences** by which the presence of the Holy Spirit in a man's heart may be known.

I. The first point I propose to consider is **the importance attached to the work of the Holy Spirit in Scripture.** I find it hard to know where to begin and where to leave off, in handling this branch of my subject. It would be easy to fill up all this paper by quoting texts about it. So often is the Holy Spirit mentioned in the New Testament, that my difficulty is not so much the discovery of evidence, as the selection of texts. Eighteen times in the eighth chapter of the Epistle to the Romans Paul speaks of God the Spirit. In fact the place which the Holy Spirit holds in the minds of most professing Christians bears no proportion to the place which He holds in the Word of God.

"There is a general omission in the saints of God, in their not giving the Holy Spirit that glory which is due to His person, and for His great work of salvation in us; insomuch that we have in our hearts almost lost this Third Person. We give daily in our thoughts, prayers, affections and speeches, an honor to the Father and the Son. But who directs the aims of his praise (more than in that general way of doxology we use to close our prayers with) unto God the Holy Spirit? He is a Person in the Godhead, equal with the Father and the Son. The work He does for us, in its kind, is as great as those of the Father or the Son. Therefore, by the equity of all law, a proportionate honor is due to Him."—Thomas Goodwin on the Work of the Holy Spirit. 1704.

I shall not spend much time in proving the divinity and personality of the Holy Spirit. They are points which are written in Scripture as with a sun-beam. I am utterly at a loss to understand how any honest-minded reader of the Bible can fail to see them. Above all, I am unable to comprehend how any unprejudiced reader of the Bible can regard the Spirit as nothing more than "an influence or principle." We find it written in the New Testament, that the Holy Spirit was "seen descending in a bodily shape." (Luke 3:22.) He commanded disciples to do acts, and lifted them through the air by His own power. (Acts 8:29-39.) He sent forth the first preachers to the Gentiles. (Acts 13:2.) He spoke to the Churches. (Rev. 2:7.) He makes intercession. (Rom. 8:26.) He searches all things, teaches all things, and guides into all truth. (1 Cor. 2:10; John 14:26; 16:13.) He is another Comforter distinct from Christ. (John 14:16.) He has personal affections ascribed to Him. (Isaiah 63:10; Ephes. 4:30; Rom. 15:30.) He has a mind, will, and power of His own. (Rom. 8:27; 1 Cor. 12:11; Rom. 15:13.) He has baptism administered in His name together with the Father and the Son. (Matt. 28:19.) And whoever shall blaspheme Him has never forgiveness, and is in danger of eternal damnation. (Mark 3:29.)

I make no comment on these passages. They speak for themselves. I only use the words of Ambrose Serle in saying, that "Two and two making four, does not appear more clear and conclusive than that the Holy Spirit is a living divine Agent, working with consciousness, will, and power. If people will not be persuaded by these testimonies, neither would they be persuaded though one rose from the dead."

I repeat that I will not spend time in dwelling on proofs of the Holy Spirit's divinity and personality. I will rather confine all I have to say on this branch of my subject to two general remarks.

For one thing, I ask my readers to remark carefully that **in every step of the grand work of man's redemption the Bible assigns a prominent place to God the Holy Spirit.**

What do you think of the **incarnation** of Christ? You know we cannot over-rate its importance. Well, it is written that when our Lord was conceived of the Virgin Mary, "the Holy Spirit came upon her, and the power of the Highest overshadowed her." (Luke 1:35.)

What do you think of the **earthly ministry** of our Lord Jesus Christ? You know that none ever did what He did, lived as He lived, and spoke as He spoke. Well, it is written that the Spirit "descended from heaven like a dove and abode upon Him,"—that "God anointed Him with the Holy Spirit,"—that "the Father gave not the Spirit by measure unto Him," and that He was "full of the Holy Spirit." (John 1:32; Acts 10:38; John 3:34; Luke 4:1.)

What do you think of the vicarious **sacrifice** of Christ on the cross? Its value is simply unspeakable. No wonder Paul says, "God forbid that I should boast, except in the cross." (Gal. 6:14.) Well, it is written, "Through the eternal Spirit He offered Himself without spot to God." (Heb. 9:14.)

What do you think of the **resurrection** of Christ? It was the seal and top-stone of all His work. He was "raised again for our justification." (Rom. 4:25.) Well, it is written that "He was put to death in the flesh—but quickened by the Spirit." (1 Pet. 3:18.)

What do you think of the **departure** of Christ from this world, when He ascended up into heaven? It was a tremendous trial to His disciples. They were left like a little orphan family, in the midst of cruel enemies. Well, what was the grand promise wherewith our Savior cheered them the night before He died? "I will ask the Father and He shall give you another Comforter, even the Spirit of truth" (John 14:16, 17.)

What do you think of the mission of the **apostles** to preach the Gospel? We Gentiles owe to it all our religious light and knowledge. Well, they were obliged to tarry at Jerusalem and "wait for the promise of the Father." They were unfit to go forth until they were "filled with the Holy Spirit," upon the day of Pentecost. (Acts 1:4; 2:4.)

What do you think of the **Scripture**, which is written for our learning? You know that our earth without a sun would be but a faint emblem of a world without a Bible. Well, we are informed that in writing that Scripture, "Holy men spoke as they were moved by the Holy Spirit." (2 Pet. 1:21.) "The things which we speak," says Paul, we speak in the words which the Holy Spirit teaches." (1 Cor. 2:13.)

What do you think of the whole dispensation under which we Christians live? You know its privileges as far exceed those of the Jews as twilight is exceeded by noonday. Well, we are especially told that it is the "ministration of the Spirit." (2 Cor. 3:8.)

I would not for a moment have anyone suppose that I think Old Testament believers had not the Holy Spirit. On the contrary I hold that there has never been a whit of spiritual life among people, excepting from the Holy Spirit—and that the Holy Spirit made Abel and Noah what they were, no less really than He made Paul. All I mean to assert is, that the Holy Spirit is so much more fully revealed and largely poured out under the New Testament than under the Old, that the New Testament dispensation is emphatically and peculiarly called the "ministration of the Spirit." The difference between the two dispensations is only one of degree.

I place these texts before my readers as matter for private meditation. I pass on to the other general remark I promised to make.

I ask you then to remark carefully, that **whatever individual Christians have, are, and enjoy, in contradistinction to the worldly and unconverted, they owe to the agency of God the Holy Spirit**. By Him they are first called, quickened, and made alive. By Him they are born again, and made new creatures. By Him they are convinced of sin, guided into all truth and led to Christ. By Him they are sealed unto the day of redemption. He dwells in them as His living temples. He witnesses with their spirits—gives them the spirit of adoption, makes them to cry 'Abba Father', and makes intercession for them. By Him they are sanctified. By Him the love of God is shed abroad in their hearts. Through His power they abound in hope. Through Him they wait for the hope of righteousness by faith. Through Him they mortify the deeds of their bodies. After Him they walk. In Him they live. In a word, all that believers have from grace to glory—all that they are from the first moment they believe to the day they depart to be with Christ—all, all, all may be traced to the work of God the Holy Spirit. (John 6:63; 3:8; 16:9, 10; Eph. 4:30; 1 Cor. 6:19; Rom. 8:15, 16, 26; 2 Thess. 2:13; Rom. 5:5; 15:13; Gal. 5:5, 25; Rom. 8:1, 13.)

I may not tarry longer on this branch of my subject. I trust I have said enough to prove that I did not use words without meaning, when I spoke of the importance attached in Scripture to the work of the Spirit of God.

Before I pass on let me entreat all who read this paper to make sure that they hold sound doctrine concerning the work of the Holy Spirit. Give Him the honor due unto His name. Give Him in your religion the place and the dignity which Scripture assigns to Him. Settle it in your minds that the work of all three Persons in the blessed Trinity, is absolutely and equally needful to the salvation of every saved soul. The election of God the Father, and the atoning blood of God the Son, are the foundation stones of our faith. But from them must never be separated the applicatory work of God the Holy Spirit. The Father chooses. The Son mediates, absolves, justifies, and intercedes. The Holy Spirit applies the whole work to man's soul. Always together in Scripture, never separated in Scripture, let the offices of the three Persons in the Trinity never be wrenched asunder and disjoined in your Christianity. What God has so beautifully joined together let no man dare to put asunder.

"To give the Holy Spirit divine worship, if he be not God, is idolatry; and to withhold it, if He is God, is a heinous sin. To be well informed on

this point, is of the greatest importance."—Hurrion on the Holy Spirit.
1731.

Accept a brotherly caution against all kinds of Christian teaching,
falsely so called—which, either directly or indirectly, dishonor the work
of the Holy Spirit. Beware of the error, on one side, which practically
substitutes church membership and participation of the sacraments for
the Spirit. Let no man make you believe that to be baptized and go to the
Lord's Table, is any sure proof that you have the Spirit of Christ. Beware
of the error, on the other side, which proudly substitutes the inward
light, so called, and the scraps of conscience which remain in every man
after the fall, for the saving grace of the Holy Spirit. Let no man make you
believe that as a matter of course, since Christ died, all men and women
have within them the Spirit of Christ. I touch on these points gently. I
would be sorry to write one needless word of controversy. But I do say
to everyone who prizes real Christianity in these days, "Be very jealous
about the real work and office of the third Person of the Trinity." Test the
spirits, to see whether they are of God. Prove diligently the many divers
and strange doctrines which now infect the Church. And let the subject
brought before you this day be one of your principal tests. Test every new
doctrine of these latter times by two simple questions. Ask first, "Where
is the Lamb?" And ask secondly, "Where is the Holy Spirit?"

"It is not the natural light of conscience, nor that improved by the
Word, which converts any man to God, although this is the best spring
of most men's practical part of religion. But it is faith, bringing in a
new light into conscience, and so conscience lighting its candle-light at
that sun which humbles for sin in another manner, and drives people
to Christ, sanctifies, changes, and writes the law in the heart. And this
you will find to be the state of difference between Augustine, and the
Pelagians, and semi-Pelagians, which the whole stream and current of

his writings against them hold forth. They would have had the light of natural conscience, and the seeds of natural virtues in people (as in philosophers), being improved by the revelation of the Word, to be that grace which the Scripture speaks of. He proclaims all their virtues, and their use of natural light to be sins, because deficient of holiness, and requires for us not only the revelation of the objects of faith, which else natural light could not find out—but a new light to see them withal."

—Thomas Goodwin on the Work of the Holy Spirit. 1704.

II. The second point I propose to consider, is **the necessity of the work of the Holy Spirit to man's salvation.**

I invite special attention to this part of the subject. Let it be a settled thing in our minds that the matter we are considering in this paper is no mere speculative question in religion, about which it signifies little what we believe. On the contrary, it lies at the very foundation of all saving Christianity. Wrong about the Holy Spirit and His offices—and we are wrong to all eternity!

The necessity of the work of the Holy Spirit arises from the total corruption of human nature. We are all by nature "dead in sins." (Eph. 2:1.) However shrewd, and clever, and wise in the things of this world, we are all dead towards God. The eyes of our understanding are blinded. We see nothing aright. Our wills, affections, and inclinations are alienated from Him who made us. "The carnal mind is enmity against God." (Rom. 8:7.) We have naturally neither faith, nor fear, nor love, nor holiness. In short, left to ourselves, we would never be saved.

Without the Holy Spirit no man ever turns to God, repents, believes, and obeys. Intellectual training and secular education alone make no true Christians. Acquaintance with fine arts and science leads no one to heaven. Pictures and statues never brought one soul to God. The "tender strokes of art" never prepared any man or woman for the judgment day.

They bind up no broken heart; they heal no wounded conscience. The Greeks had their Zeuxis and Parrhasius, their Phidias and Praxiteles, masters as great in their day as any in modern times; yet the Greeks knew nothing of the way of peace with God. They were sunk in gross idolatry, and bowed down to the works of their own hands. The most zealous efforts of ministers alone cannot make people Christians. The ablest scriptural reasoning has no effect on the mind; the most fervent pulpit eloquence will not move the heart; the naked truth alone will not lead the will. We who are ministers know this well by painful experience. We can show people the fountain of living waters—but we cannot make them drink. We see many a one sitting under our pulpits year after year, and hearing hundreds of sermons, full of Gospel truth, without the slightest result. We mark him year after year, unaffected and unmoved by every Scriptural argument—cold as the stones on which he treads as he enters our church, unmoved as the marble statue which adorns the tomb against the wall—dead as the old dry oak of which his pew is made, feelingless as the painted glass in the windows, through which the sun shines on his head. We look at him with wonder and sorrow, and remember Xavier's words as he looked at China, "Oh, rock, rock! when will you open?" And we learn by such cases as these, that nothing will make a Christian but the introduction into the heart of a new nature, a new principle, and a Divine seed from above.

What is it then that man needs? We need to be "born again," and this new birth we must receive of the Holy Spirit. The Spirit of life must quicken us. The Spirit must renew us. The Spirit must take away from us the heart of stone. The Spirit must put in us the heart of flesh. A new act of creation must take place. A new being must be called into existence. Without all this we cannot be saved. Here lies the main part of our need of the Holy Spirit. "Except a man be born again he cannot see the kingdom of God." (John 3:3.) No salvation without a new birth!

"This is that which gives unto the ministry of the Gospel both its glory and its efficacy. Take away the Spirit from the Gospel, and you render it a dead letter, and leave the New Testament of no more use unto Christians than the Old Testament is unto the Jews."—Owen on the Holy Spirit.

"In the power of the Holy Spirit rests all ability to know God and to please Him. It is He who purifies the mind by His secret working. He enlightens the mind to conceive worthy thoughts of Almighty God."—Homily

Let us dismiss from our minds forever the common idea that natural theology, moral persuasion, logical arguments, or even an exhibition of Gospel truth, are sufficient of themselves to turn a sinner from his sins, if once brought to bear upon him. It is a strong delusion. They will not do so. The heart of man is far harder than we fancy—the 'old Adam' is much more strong than we suppose. The ships which run aground at half-ebb, will never stir until the tide flows—the heart of man will never look to Christ, repent, and believe, until the Holy Spirit comes down upon it. Until that takes place, our inner nature is like the earth before the present order of creation began, "without form and void, and darkness covering the face of the deep." (Gen. 1:2.) The same power which said at the beginning, "Let there be light—and there was light," must work a creating work in us, or we shall never rise to newness of life.

But I have something more to say yet on this branch of my subject. The necessity of the work of the Spirit to man's salvation is a wide field, and I have yet another remark to make upon it.

I say then, that **without the work of the Holy Spirit no man could ever be fit to dwell with God in another world**. A fitness of some kind we must have. The mere pardon of our sins would be a worthless gift, unless accompanied by the gift of a new nature, a nature in harmony and in tune with that of God Himself. We need a **fitness** for heaven, as well as a **title** for heaven, and this fitness we must receive from the Holy Spirit. We must be made "partakers of the divine nature," by the indwelling of the Holy Spirit. (2 Pet. 1:4.) The Spirit must sanctify our carnal natures, and make them love spiritual things. The Spirit must wean our affections from things below, and teach us to set them on things above. The Spirit must bend our stubborn wills, and teach them to be submissive to the will of God. The Spirit must write again the law of God on our inward man, and put His fear within us. The Spirit must transform us by the daily renewing of our minds, and implant in us the image of Him whose servants we profess to be. Here lies the other great part of our need of the Holy Spirit's work. We need sanctification no less than justification, "Without holiness no man shall see the Lord." (Heb. 12:14.)

Once more I beseech my readers to dismiss from their minds the common idea, that men and women need nothing but pardon and absolution, in order to be prepared to meet God. It is a strong delusion, and one against which I desire with all my heart to place you on your guard. It is not enough, as many a poor ignorant Christian supposes on his death-bed, if God "pardons our sins and takes us to rest." I say again most emphatically, it is not enough. The love of sin must be taken from us, as well as the guilt of sin removed; the desire of pleasing God must be implanted in us, as well as the fear of God's judgment taken away; a love to holiness must be engrafted, as well as a dread of punishment removed. Heaven itself would be no heaven to us if we entered it without a new heart.

An eternal Sabbath and the society of saints and angels could give us no happiness in heaven, unless the love of Sabbaths and of holy company had been first shed abroad in our hearts upon earth. Whether people will hear or forbear, the man who enters heaven must have the sanctification of the Spirit, as well as the sprinkling of the blood of Jesus Christ. To use the words of Owen, "When God designed the great and glorious work of recovering fallen man and saving sinners, He appointed in His infinite wisdom two great means. The one was the giving of His Son for them; and the other was the giving of his Spirit unto them. And hereby was way made for the manifestation of the glory of the whole blessed Trinity."

"God the Father had but two grand gifts to bestow; and when once they were given, He had left then nothing that was great (comparatively) to give, for they contained all good in them. These two gifts were His Son, who was His promise in the Old Testament, and the Spirit, the promise of the New."—Thomas Goodwin on the Work of the Holy Spirit. 1704.

I trust I have said enough to show the absolute necessity of the work of the Holy Spirit to the salvation of man's soul. Man's utter inability to turn to God without the Spirit—man's utter unfitness for the joys of heaven, without the Spirit—are two great foundation stones in revealed religion, which ought to be always deeply rooted in a Christian's mind. Rightly understood, they will lead to one conclusion, "Without the Spirit, no salvation!"

Would you like to know the reason why we who preach the Gospel, preach so often about conversion? We do it because of the necessities of men's souls. We do it because we see plainly from the Word of God that nothing short of a thorough change of heart will ever meet the exigencies of your case. Your case is naturally desperate. Your danger is great. **You need not only the atonement of Jesus Christ—but the quickening, sanctifying work of the Holy Spirit, to make you a true Christian, and deliver you from hell.** Gladly would I lead to heaven all who read this volume! My heart's desire and prayer to God is that you may be saved. But I know that none enter heaven without a heart to enjoy heaven, and this heart we must receive from God's Spirit.

Shall I tell you plainly the reason why some receive these truths so coldly, and are so little affected by them? You hear us listless and unconcerned. You think us extreme and extravagant in our statements. And why is this? It is just because you do not see or know the disease of your own soul. You are not aware of your own sinfulness and weakness. **Low and inadequate views of your spiritual disease, are sure to be accompanied by low and inadequate views of the remedy provided in the Gospel.** What shall I say to you? I can only say, "May the Lord awaken you! May the Lord have mercy on your soul!" The day may come when the scales will fall from your eyes, when old things will pass away, and all things become new. And in that day I foretell and forewarn you confidently that the first truth you will grasp, next to the work of Christ, will be the absolute necessity of the work of the Holy Spirit.

III. The third thing I propose to consider, is **the Manner in which the Holy Spirit works on the hearts of those who are saved.**

I approach this branch of my subject with much difficulty. I am very sensible that it is surrounded with difficulties, and involves many of the deepest things of God. But it is folly for mortal man to turn away from any truth in Christianity, merely because of difficulties. Better a thousand times receive with meekness what we cannot fully explain, and believe that what we know not now, we shall know hereafter. "Enough for us," says an old divine, "if we sit in God's court, without pretending to be of God's counsel."

In speaking of the manner of the Holy Spirit's working, I shall simply state certain great leading facts. They are facts attested alike by Scripture and experience. They are facts patent to the eyes of every candid and well instructed observer. They are facts which I believe it is impossible to gainsay.

(a) I say then that the Holy Spirit works on the heart of a man in a mysterious manner. Our Lord Jesus Christ Himself tell us that in well-known words, "The wind blows where it wills, and you hear the sound thereof—but cannot tell whence it comes and where it goes; so is everyone that is born of the Spirit." (John 3:8.) We cannot explain how and in what way the Almighty Spirit comes into man, and operates upon him; but neither also can we explain a thousand things which are continually taking place in the natural world. We cannot explain how our wills work daily on our bodily members, and make them walk, or move, or rest, at our discretion; yet no one ever thinks of disputing the fact. So ought it to be with the work of the Spirit. We ought to believe the fact, though we cannot explain the manner.

(b) I say furthermore, that the Holy Spirit works on the heart of a man in a sovereign manner. He comes to one and does not come to another. He often converts one in a family, while others are left alone. There were two thieves crucified with our Lord Jesus Christ on Calvary. They saw the same Savior dying, and heard the same words come from His lips. Yet only one repented and went to Paradise, while the other died in his sins. There were many Pharisees besides Saul, who had a hand in Stephen's murder; but Saul alone became an apostle. There were many slave captains in John Newton's time; yet none but he became a preacher of the Gospel. We cannot account for this. But neither can we account for China being a heathen country, and England a Christian land—we only know that so it is.

(c) I say furthermore, that the Holy Spirit always works on the heart of a man in such a manner as to be felt . I do not for a moment say that the feelings which He produces are always understood by the person in whom they are produced. On the contrary, they are often a cause of anxiety, and conflict, and inward strife. All I maintain is that we have no warrant of Scripture for supposing that there is an indwelling of the Spirit which is not felt at all. Where He is, there will always be corresponding feelings.

(d) I say furthermore, that the Holy Spirit always works on the heart of a man in such a manner as to be Seen in the man's life. I do not say that as soon as He comes into a man, that man becomes immediately an established Christian, a Christian in whose life and ways nothing but spirituality can be observed. But this I say—that **the Almighty Spirit is never present in a person's soul without producing some perceptible results in that person's conduct!** He never sleeps—He is never idle. We have no warrant of Scripture for talking of "dormant grace." "Whoever is born of God does not commit sin; for his seed remains in him." (1 John 3:9.) Where the Holy Spirit is, there will be something seen.

(e) I say furthermore, that the Holy Spirit always works on the heart of a man in an irresistible manner. I do not deny for a moment that there are sometimes spiritual strivings and workings of conscience in the minds of unconverted people, which finally come to nothing. But I say confidently, that when the Spirit really begins a work of conversion, He always carries that work to perfection. He effects miraculous changes. He turns the character upside down. He causes old things to pass away, and all things to become new. In a word, the Holy Spirit is Almighty. With Him nothing is impossible.

(f) I say, finally, under this head, that the Holy Spirit generally works on the heart of man through the use of means. The Word of God, preached or read, is generally employed by Him as an instrument in the conversion of a soul. He applies that Word to the conscience—He brings that Word home to the mind. This is His general course of procedure. There are instances, undoubtedly, in which people are converted "without the Word." (1 Pet. 3:1.) But, as a general rule, God's truth is the sword of the Spirit. By it He teaches, and teaches nothing else but that which is written in the Word.

I commend these six points to the attention of all my readers. A right understanding of them supplies the best antidote to the many false and spurious doctrines by which Satan labors to darken the blessed work of the Spirit.

(a) Is there **a haughty, high-minded person** reading this paper, who in his pride of intellect rejects the work of the Holy Spirit, because of its mysteriousness and sovereignty? I tell you boldly that you must take up other ground than this before you dispute and deny our doctrine. Look to the heaven above you, and the earth beneath you, and deny, if you can, that there are mysteries there. Look to the map of the world you live in, and the marvelous difference between the privileges of one nation and another, and deny if you can, that there is sovereignty there. Go and learn to be consistent. Submit that proud mind of yours to plain undeniable facts. Be clothed with the humility that befits poor mortal man. Cast off that affectation of reasoning, under which you now try to smother your conscience. Dare to confess that the work of the Spirit may be mysterious and sovereign, and yet for all that is true.

(b) Is there **a Romanist, or semi-Romanist** reading this paper, who tries to persuade himself that all baptized people, and members of the Church, as a matter of course, have the Spirit? I tell you plainly that you are deceiving yourself, if you dream that the Spirit is in a man, when His presence cannot be seen. Go and learn this day that the presence of the Holy Spirit is to be tested, not by the name in the register, or the place in the family pew—but by the visible fruits in a man's life.

(c) Is there a **worldly man** reading this paper, who regards all claims to the indwelling of the Spirit as so much enthusiasm and fanaticism? I warn you also to take heed what you are about. No doubt there is plenty of hypocrisy and false profession in the Churches; no doubt there are thousands whose religious feelings are mere delusion. But counterfeit money is no proof that there is no such thing as good coin—**the abuse of a thing does not destroy the use of it.** The Bible tells us plainly that there are certain hopes, and joys, and sorrows, and inward feelings, inseparable from the work of the Spirit of God. Go and learn this day that you have not received the Spirit, if His presence within you has not been felt.

(d) Is there an **excuse-making indolent person** reading this paper, who comforts himself with the thought that decided Christianity is an impossible thing, and that in a world like this he cannot serve Christ? Your excuses will not avail you. The power of the Holy Spirit is offered to you without money and without price. Go and learn this day that there is strength to be had for the asking. Through the Spirit, whom the Lord Jesus offers to give to you, all difficulties may be overcome.

(e) Is there a fanatic reading this paper, who fancies that it matters nothing whether a man stays at home or goes to church, and that if a man is to be saved, he will be saved in spite of himself? I tell you also this day, that you have much to learn. Go and learn that the Holy Spirit ordinarily works through the use of means of grace, and that it is by "hearing" that faith generally comes into the soul." (Rom. 10:17.)

I leave this branch of my subject here, and pass on. I leave it with a sorrowful conviction that nothing in religion so shows the blindness of natural man as his inability to receive the teaching of Scripture on the manner of the Holy Spirit's operations. To quote the saying of our Divine Master, "The world cannot receive Him." (John 14:17.) To use the words of Ambrose Serle, "This operation of the Spirit has been, and ever will be, an incomprehensible business to those who have not known it in themselves. Like Nicodemus, and other masters in Israel, they will reason and re-reason, until they puzzle and perplex themselves, by darkening counsel without knowledge; and when they cannot make out the matter, will give the strongest proof of all that they know nothing of it, by fretting and raving, and calling hard names, and saying, in short, that there is no such thing."

IV. I propose, in the last place, to consider the marks and evidences by which the presence of the Holy Spirit in a man's heart may be known.

Last as this point comes in order, it is anything but last in importance. In fact, it is that view of the Holy Spirit which demands the closest attention of every professing Christian. We have seen something of the place assigned to the Holy Spirit in the Bible. We have seen something of the absolute necessity of the Holy Spirit to a man's salvation. We have seen something of the manner of the Holy Spirit's operations. And now comes the mighty question, which ought to interest every reader, "How are we to know whether we are partakers of the Holy Spirit? By what marks may we find out whether we have the Spirit of Christ?"

I will begin by taking it for granted that the question I have just asked may be answered. Where is the use of our Bibles, if we cannot find out whether we are in the way to heaven? Let it be a settled principle in our Christianity, that a man may know whether or not he has the Holy Spirit. Let us dismiss from our minds once and forever the many unscriptural evidences of the Spirit's presence with which thousands content themselves. Reception of the sacraments and membership of the visible Church are no proofs whatever that we "have the Spirit of Christ."

In short, I call it a shortcut to the grossest antinomianism to talk of a man having the Holy Spirit—so long as he serves sin and the world.

The presence of the Holy Spirit in a man's heart can only be known by the fruits and effects He produces. Mysterious and invisible to mortal eye as His operations are, they always lead to certain visible and tangible results. Just as you know the compass-needle to be magnetized by its turning to the north—just as you know there is life in a tree by its sap, buds, leaves and fruits—just as you know there is a steersman on board a ship by its keeping a steady regular course—just so you may know the Spirit to be in a man's heart by the influence He exercises over his thoughts, affections, opinions, habits, and life. I lay this down broadly and unhesitatingly. I find no safe ground to occupy excepting this. I see no safeguard against the wildest enthusiasm, excepting in this position. And I see it clearly marked out in our Lord Jesus Christ's words, "Every tree is known by his own fruit." (Luke 6:44.)

But what are the specific fruits by which the presence of the Spirit in the heart may be known? I find no difficulty in answering that question. The Holy Spirit always works after a certain definite pattern. Just as the bee always forms the cells of its comb in one regular hexagonal shape, so does the Spirit of God work on the heart of man with one uniform result. His work is the work of a master. The world may see no beauty in it—it is foolishness to the natural man. But "he who is spiritual discerns all things." (1 Cor. 2:15.) A well-instructed Christian knows well the fruits of the Spirit of God. Let me briefly set them before you in order. They are all clear and unmistakable, "plain to him who understands, and right to those who find knowledge." (Prov. 8:9.)

(1) Where the Holy Spirit is, there will always be **deep conviction of sin, and true repentance for it.** It is His special office to convince of sin. (John 16:8.) He shows the exceeding holiness of God. He teaches

the exceeding corruption and infirmity of our nature. He strips us of our blind self-righteousness. He opens our eyes to our awful guilt, folly and danger. He fills the heart with sorrow, contrition, and abhorrence for sin, as the abominable thing which God hates. He who knows nothing of all this, and saunters carelessly through life, thoughtless about sin, and indifferent and unconcerned about his soul, is a dead man before God! He has not the Spirit of Christ.

(2) Where the Holy Spirit is, there will always be **lively faith in Jesus Christ, as the only Savior**. It is His special office to testify of Christ, to take of the things of Christ and show them to man. (John 16:15.) He leads the soul which feels its sin, to Jesus and the atonement made by His blood. He shows the soul that Christ has suffered for sin, the just for the unjust, to bring us to God. He points out to the sin-sick soul that we have only to receive Christ, believe in Christ, commit ourselves to Christ, and pardon, peace, and life eternal, are at once our own. He makes us see a beautiful fitness in Christ's finished work of redemption to meet our spiritual necessities. He makes us willing to disclaim all merit of our own and to venture all on Jesus, looking to nothing, resting on nothing, trusting in nothing but Christ, Christ, "delivered for our offences, and raised again for our justification." (Rom. 4:25.) He who knows nothing of all this, and builds on any other foundation, is dead before God. He has not the Spirit of Christ.

(3) Where the Holy Spirit is, there will always be **holiness of life and conversation**. He is the Spirit of holiness. (Rom. 1:4.) He is the sanctifying Spirit. He takes away the hard, carnal, worldly heart of man, and puts in its place a tender, conscientious, spiritual heart, delighting in the Word of God. He makes a man turn his face towards God, and desire above all things to please Him, and turn his back on the fashion of this world, and no longer make that fashion his God. He sows in a man's

heart the blessed seeds of "love, joy, meekness, longsuffering, gentleness, goodness, faith, temperance," and causes these seeds to spring up and bear pleasant fruit. (Gal. 5:22.) He who lacks these things, and knows nothing of daily practical godliness, is dead before God. He has not the Spirit of Christ.

(4) Where the Holy Spirit is, there will always be **the habit of earnest private prayer**. He is the Spirit of grace and supplication. (Zech. 12:10.) He works in the heart as the Spirit of adoption, whereby we cry Abba, Father. He makes a man feel that he must cry to God, and speak to God—feebly, falteringly, weakly, it may be—but cry he must about his soul. He makes it as natural to a man to pray as it is to an infant to breathe; with this one difference—that the infant breathes without an effort, and the new-born soul prays with much conflict and strife. He who knows nothing of real, living, fervent, private prayer, and is content with some old form, or with no prayer at all—is dead before God. He has not the Spirit of Christ.

(5) Finally, where the Holy Spirit is, there will always be **love and reverence for God's Word**. He makes the new-born soul desire the sincere milk of the Word, just as the infant desires its natural food. He makes it "delight in the law of the Lord." (1 Pet. 2:2; Psalm. 1:2.) He shows man a fullness, and depth, and wisdom, and sufficiency, in the Holy Scripture, which is utterly hid from a natural man's eyes. He draws him to the Word with an irresistible force, as the light and lantern, and manna, and sword, which are essential to a safe journey through this world. If the man cannot read He makes him love to hear—if he cannot hear He makes him love to meditate. But to the Word the Spirit always leads him. He who sees no special beauty in God's Bible, and takes no pleasure in reading, hearing, and understanding it, is dead before God. He has not the Spirit of Christ.

I place these five grand marks of the Spirit's presence before my readers, and confidently claim attention to them. I believe they will bear inspection. I am not afraid of their being searched, criticized, and cross-examined. Repentance toward God—faith toward our Lord Jesus Christ—holiness of heart and life—habits of real private prayer—love and reverence toward God's Word—these are the real proofs of the indwelling of the Holy Spirit in a man's soul. Where He is, these marks will be seen. Where He is not, these marks will be lacking.

I grant freely that the leadings of the Spirit, in some minute details, are not always uniform. The paths over which He conducts souls, are not always precisely one and the same. The experience that true Christians pass through in their beginnings is often somewhat various. This only I maintain—that the main road into which the Spirit leads people, and the final results which He at length produces, are always alike. In all true Christians, the five great marks I have already mentioned will always be found.

I grant freely that **the degree and depth of the work of the Spirit in the heart may vary exceedingly.** There is weak faith and strong faith—weak love and strong love—a bright hope and a dim hope—a feeble obedience to Christ's will, and a close following of the Lord. This only I maintain—that the main outlines of religious character in all who have the Spirit, perfectly correspond. Life is life, whether strong or feeble. The infant in arms, though weak and dependent, is as real and true a representative of the great family of Adam as the strongest man alive.

Wherever you see these five great marks, you see a true Christian. Let that never be forgotten. I leave it to others to excommunicate and unchurch all who do not belong to their own denomination, and do not worship after their own particular fashion. I have no sympathy with such narrow-mindedness. Show me a man who repents, and believes in Christ crucified—who lives a holy life, and delights in his Bible and prayer—and I desire to regard him as a brother. I see in him a member of the universal Christian Church, out of which there is no salvation. I behold in him an heir of that crown of glory which is incorruptible and fades not away. If he has the Holy Spirit, he has Christ. If he has Christ, he has God. If he has God the Father, God the Son, and God the Spirit, all things are his. Who am I that I should turn my back on him, because we cannot see all things eye to eye?

Wherever these five great marks of the Spirit are lacking, we have just cause to be afraid about a man's soul. Visible Churches may endorse him, sacraments may be administered to him, forms of prayer may be read over him, ministers may charitably speak of him as "a brother," but all this does not alter the real state of things. The man is in the broad way that leads to destruction. Without the Spirit he is without Christ. Without Christ he is without God. Without God the Father, God the Son, and God the Spirit, he is in imminent danger. The Lord have mercy upon his soul!

I hasten on now towards a conclusion. I desire to wind up all I have been saying by a few words of direct **personal application.**

(1) In the first place, let me ask a question of all who read this paper. It is a short and simple one, and grows naturally out of the subject. "Have you, or have you not, the Spirit of Christ?"

I am not afraid to ask this question. I will not be stopped by the commonplace remark that it is absurd, enthusiastic, unreasonable to ask such questions in the present day. I take my stand on a plain declaration or Scripture. I find an inspired Apostle saying, "If anyone does not have the Spirit of Christ, he does not belong to Him." I want to know what can be more reasonable than to press on your conscience the inquiry, "Have you the Spirit of Christ?"

I will not be stopped by the foolish observation, that no man can tell in this world whether or not he has the Spirit. No man can tell! Then what was the Bible given to us for? What is the use of the Scriptures if we cannot discover whether we are going to heaven or hell? The thing I ask can be known. The evidences of the Spirit's presence in the soul are simple, plain, and intelligible. No honest inquirer needs miss the way in this matter. You may find out whether you have the Holy Spirit.

I entreat you not to evade the question I have now asked. I beseech you to allow it to work inwardly in your heart. I charge you, as ever you would be saved, to give it an honest answer. Baptism, Church-membership, respectability, morality, outward correctness, are all excellent things. But do not be content with them. Go deeper—look further. "Have you received the Holy Spirit? Have you the Spirit of Christ?"

"It is a good sign of grace when a man is willing to search and examine himself, whether he is gracious or not. There is a certain instinct in a child of God, whereby be naturally desires to have the title of his legitimation tried; whereas a hypocrite dreads nothing more than to have his rottenness searched into."—Hopkins.

(2) Let me, in the next place, offer a solemn warning to all who feel in their own consciences that they have not the Spirit of Christ. That warning is short and simple. If you have not the Spirit, you are not yet Christ's people—you are "none of His."

Think for a moment how much is involved in those few words, "none of His." You are not washed in Christ's blood! You are not clothed in His righteousness! You are not justified! You are not interceded for! Your sins are yet upon you! The devil claims you for his own! The pit opens her mouth for you! The torments of hell wait for you!

I have no desire to create needless fear. I only want sensible people to look calmly at things as they are. I only want one plain text of Scripture to be duly weighed. It is written, "If any man has not the Spirit of Christ, he is none of His." And I say in the sight of such a text, if you die without the Spirit, it would have been better if you never had been born.

(3) Let me, in the next place, give an earnest invitation to all who feel that they have not the Spirit. That invitation is short and simple. Go and cry to God this day in the name of the Lord Jesus Christ, and pray for the Holy Spirit to be poured down on your soul. There is every possible encouragement to do this. There is warrant of Scripture for doing it. "Turn at my reproof, I will pour out my Spirit upon you. I will make known my words unto you." "If you, being evil, know how to give good gifts to your children, how much more shall your heavenly Father give the Holy Spirit to those who ask Him." (Prov. 1:23; Luke 11:13.) There is warrant in the experience of thousands for doing it. Thousands will rise at the last day, and testify that when they prayed they were heard, and when they sought grace, they found it. Above all, there is warrant in the person and character of our Lord Jesus Christ. He waits to be gracious. He invites sinners to come to Him. He rejects none that come. He gives "power to all who receive Him by faith and come to Him, to become the sons of God." (John 1:12.)

Go then to Jesus, as a needy, wanting, humble, contrite sinner, and you shall not go in vain. Cry to Him mightily about your soul, and you shall not cry to no purpose. Confess to Him your need, and guilt, and fear, and danger, and He will not despise you. Ask, and you shall receive. Seek, and you shall find. Knock, and it shall be opened to you. I testify to the chief of sinners this day, that there is enough in Christ, and to spare, for your soul. Come, come—come, this very day. Come to Christ!

(4) Let me, in the last place, give a parting word of **exhortation** to all readers of this paper who have received the Spirit of Christ—to the

penitent, the believing, the holy, the praying, the lovers of the Word of God. That exhortation shall consist of three simple things.

(a) For one thing, **be thankful for the Spirit**. Who has made you to differ? Whence came all these feeling in your heart, which thousands around you know not, and you yourself knew not at one time? To what do you owe that sense of sin, and that drawing towards Christ, and that hunger and thirst after righteousness, and that taste for the Bible and prayer, which, with all your doubts and infirmities, you find within your soul? Did these things come of nature? Oh, no! Did you learn these things in the schools of this world? Oh, no! no! They are all of grace. Grace sowed them, grace watered them, grace began them, grace has kept them up. Learn to be more thankful. Praise God more every day you live—praise Him more in private, praise Him more in public, praise Him in your own family, praise Him above all in your own heart. This is the way to be in tune for heaven. The anthem there will be, "What has God wrought?"

(b) For another thing, **be filled with the Spirit**. Seek to be more and more under His blessed influence. Strive to have every thought, and word, and action, and habit, brought under obedience to the leadings of the Holy Spirit. Grieve Him not by inconsistencies and conformity to the world. Quench Him not by trifling with little infirmities and small besetting sins. Seek rather to have Him ruling and reigning more completely over you every week that you live. Pray that you may yearly grow in grace, and in the knowledge of Christ. This is the way to do good to the world. An eminent Christian is a light-house—seen far and wide by others, and doing good to myriads, whom he never knows. This is the way to enjoy much inward comfort in this world, to have bright assurance in death, to leave broad evidences behind us, and at last to receive a great crown.

(c) Finally, **pray daily for a great outpouring of the Spirit on the Church and on the world**. This is the grand need of the day—it is the thing that we need far more than money, machinery, and men. The "company of preachers" in Christendom is far greater than it was in the days of Paul; but the actual spiritual work done in the earth, in proportion to the means used, is undoubtedly far less. We need more of the presence of the Holy Spirit—more in the pulpit, and more in the congregation—more in the pastoral visit, and more in the school. Where He is, there will be life, health, growth, and fruitfulness. Where He is not—all will be dead, tame, formal, sleepy, and cold. Then let everyone who desires to see an increase of pure and undefiled religion, pray daily for more of the presence of the Holy Spirit in every branch of the visible Church of Christ.

Chapter Two

Regeneration

"Truly, truly, I say to you—Unless a man is born again, he cannot see the kingdom of God." John 3:3

If the Bible is false, as some proud men have dared to say—then we are no better than the beasts which perish, and the best thing a man can do is to eat and drink and live as he pleases. If the Bible is only half true, as some unhappy people strive to make out, there is no certainty about our everlasting souls; Christianity is all doubt and dimness and guesswork, we can never know what we are to believe as necessary to salvation, we can never be sure that we have got hold of the words of eternal life. Give up your Bible, and you have not a square inch of certainty and confidence to stand on: you may think, and you may imagine, and you may have your own opinion—but you cannot show me any satisfactory proof or authority that you are right; you are building merely on your own judgment; you have put out your own eyes, as it were, and, like one in the dark, you do not really know where you are going.

But if, beloved, the Bible be indeed the Word of God Himself and altogether true, and that it is so, can be proved by witnesses without number; if the Bible be indeed true and our only guide to heaven, and this I trust you are all ready to allow; it surely must be the duty of every wise and thinking man to lay to heart each doctrine which it contains, and while he adds nothing to it, to be careful that he takes nothing from it.

Now, I say that on the face of the Bible, when fairly read, there stands out this grand doctrine, that each one of us must, between the cradle and grave—go through a spiritual change, a change of heart—or in other words be born again. And in the text you have heard, the Lord Jesus declares positively, without regeneration no man shall see the kingdom of God.

Sinner, man or woman, mark that! no salvation without this new birth! Christ has done everything for you; He paid the price of our redemption, lived for us, died for us, rose again for us—but all shall avail us nothing, if there be not this work in us: *we must be born again!*

Now, beloved, I desire to speak to you freely and plainly about this new birth—as a thing absolutely necessary to salvation. I shall try to show you from my text two things: *first*, the reason why we must all be born again, and *secondly*, what the expression to be born again means; and the Lord grant that the subject to which I am going to call your attention, may not be listened to and soon forgotten, as a light and indifferent matter—but carried home and thought over, and blessed to the conversion of many souls!

I. Why, then, is this new birth so necessary? The answer is short and simple. Because of the natural sinfulness of every man's disposition. We are not born into the world with spotless, innocent minds—but corrupt and wicked, and with a will to do that which is evil as soon as we have the power. The Scriptural account is true to the letter—we are all conceived in sin and shaped in iniquity. I need not stop now to tell you how all this came to pass; I need only remind you that in the beginning it was not so. Our first parents, Adam and Eve, were created holy, harmless, undefiled, without spot or stain or blemish about them; and when God rested from His labor on the seventh day, He pronounced them, like all His other works, to be very good. But, alas for us! Adam, by transgression, fell into sin, and lost his first estate. He forfeited the likeness of God in which he had been made. And hence all we, who are his children, come into being with a defiled and sinful nature. We are fallen, and we must needs be raised; we have about us the marks of the old Adam—Adam the first, earthly and carnal—and we must needs be marked with the marks of the Second Adam, the Lord Jesus, which are heavenly and spiritual. Do any of you feel a doubt of this? Consider only what we are by nature.

By nature we do not see Christ's spiritual kingdom upon earth; it is all hidden from our eyes. Men may be sharp and knowing in worldly matters, they may be wise in the things of time—but when they come to spiritual religion, their understandings seem blind, there is a thick veil over their hearts, and they see nothing as they ought to see.

So long as they are in this natural state it is in vain they are told of God's holiness and God's unchangeable justice, His spiritual law and His judgment to come, their own enormous deficiencies, their own peril of destruction—it matters not; it all falls flat and dull upon their ears; they neither feel it nor care for it nor consider it, and in a few hours they are as though they had never heard it. It is to no purpose, while in this condition, that Christ crucified and His precious atonement are set before us; we can see no form nor beauty nor loveliness about Him; we cannot value what He has done, and, as far as we are concerned, the wisdom and the excellence of the Cross, which Apostles gloried in, seems all thrown away.

And why is this? Our hearts need changing! "The natural man receives not the things of the Spirit of God; for they are foolishness unto him; neither can he know them, for they are spiritually discerned." This is the true account of all that weariness and lifelessness and carelessness which we so often see in the worshipers of God's house; this is the secret of that awful indifference about spiritual things which prevails so widely both among rich and poor, and makes the Gospel appear a sealed book. It comes from the heart. Some always imagine they need learning, some they have no time, some they have very peculiar difficulties which no one else in the world has—but the truth lies far deeper. They all need new hearts! Once give them new natures, and you would hear no more about learning—or time—or difficulty. Every mountain would be levelled and every valley filled up, that the way of God might be prepared.

But again. By nature we do not love the laws of Christ's spiritual kingdom. We do not openly refuse to obey them, we would be angry with anyone who said we had thrown them aside—but we have no love to them and delight in them; it is not our food and drink to do our Father's will. Oh no! by nature we love our own way and our own inclinations—and that is our only law. We bring forth fruit unto ourselves—but not unto God. Our own pleasure and our own profit take up all our attention, and as for Him who made us and redeemed us, too many do not give Him the very scraps of their time. By nature we do not measure ourselves by God's standard: who ever takes the Sermon on the Mount as his rule of character? who ever admires the poor in spirit, the mourners, the meek, the hungerers and thirsters after righteousness, the merciful, the pure in heart, the peacemakers, the men who are persecuted for righteousness' sake? These are all people whom the world despises, they are as nothing by the side of the jovial and light-hearted, the men who love strong drink and are held to sing good songs; and yet these are the people whom Jesus calls blessed.

What natural man judges of sin as Jesus teaches us to judge? How few look on drunkenness and fornication as damnable sins—yet the Bible says they are! How few consider anger without cause, as bad as murder, and lustful looks as bad as adultery—yet Jesus says they are! Where are the men who strive to love their enemies, who bless those who hate them, and pray for those who despitefully use them?—yet this is the rule that Jesus has laid down. And why is all this? You see there must be something radically wrong. By nature we do not lay ourselves out to glorify God with our bodies and spirits—we take no pleasure in speaking to each other about Him. The concerns of this world have a hundred times more of our thoughts; and few indeed are the gatherings where the mention of Christ and heaven would not stop many mouths, and make nearly all look as if the subject was very uncomfortable.

And why is all this? Some talk of bad example having done them harm, and some say they have had a bad education—but the evil is far more deeply seated; that which is born of the flesh is flesh, it comes from the carnal unrenewed mind, and the remedy needed is change of nature. A corrupt tree can only bring forth corrupt fruit; the root of the mischief is the sinfulness of the natural heart.

Once more. By nature we are altogether unfit for Christ's kingdom in glory. The **lives** which we are in the habit of leading, and the **practices** we are fond of indulging, and the **tastes** we are always seeking to please, and the **opinions** we hold, are all such as prove we have no natural fitness for the inheritance of the saints in light. They do not follow after holiness in all their walk and conversation. Then what place can they occupy in that blessed abode where there shall enter in nothing that defiles, nor whatever works abomination? How shall they stand in His presence, who charges even His angels with folly, and in whose sight the very heavens are not pure! They do not take pleasure in the exercise of prayer and praise on earth; and how could they enjoy the employments of that glorious habitation, where they rest not day nor night worshiping and crying "Holy, holy, holy, Lord God Almighty, who was, and is, and is to come!"

They do not count it a privilege to draw near to God through Jesus Christ, to walk with Him, to seek close acquaintance with Him; and where would be the comfort to them of dwelling forever in the presence of the Lord God and the Lamb? They do not strive to walk in the steps of holy men of old, they do not take example from the faith and patience of the saints; and with what face then would they join the society of just men made perfect? With what salutation, after a life spent in pleasing the devil and the world, would they greet Abraham and David and the Apostles and all that blessed company who have fought the good fight?

Alas! beloved, an unregenerate man in heaven would be a miserable creature, there would be something in the air he could not breathe, the joys, the affections, the employments would be all wearisome to him, he would find himself as unfitted for the company of the saints, as a beast is unfitted on earth for the company of man. He would be carnally minded, they would be spiritually minded, there would be nothing in common. I know there are vain dreamers who imagine death will work an alteration, that they may die sinners and rise again saints—but it is all a delusion, there is no work nor device nor knowledge in the grave; if we die spiritual we shall rise spiritual, if we die carnal we shall rise carnal, and if we are to be made fit for heaven our natural hearts must be changed now on earth.

In short, beloved, the plain truth is, that by nature men are all dead in trespasses and sins, strangers to the covenant of promise, having no hope and without God in the world, prisoners in the hand of Satan, in a state of miserable condemnation, spiritually dark, blind, and dead; and, worst of all, they neither know nor feel it. The cold corpse in the grave does not feel the worms that crawl over it; the sleeping wretch who has drunk poison, does not know that he shall wake no more; and so also the unhappy man who is still unconverted cannot understand that he is in need of anything. But still, every natural man in the sight of God is dead while he lives; his body, soul, and mind are all turned aside from their proper use, which is to glorify God, and so he is looked upon as dead. And this either is the state of every single soul among us at this minute—or else it used to be. There is no middle state; we cannot be half-way, neither dead nor alive; we were dead and have been brought to life—or we are now dead, and the work is yet to be done.

Nor yet is this doctrine for publicans and harlots only: it is for all without exception; it touches high and low, rich and poor, learned and unlearned, old and young, gentle and simple; all are by nature sinful and corrupt, and because they are so, Jesus tells us solemnly not one shall enter into the heavenly rest without being born again.

Beloved, this sounds strong; it seems a hard saying, perhaps. That is not my concern. I am set to preach Christ's Gospel and not my own. Search the Scriptures, and you will see it is true.

II. The second thing for your consideration is **the exact meaning and force of that peculiar expression "to be born again."** It is a change by which we once more recover something of the divine nature, and are renewed after the image of God. It is a complete transforming and altering of all the inner man; and nothing can more fully show its completeness and importance than the strong figure under which Jesus describes it: He calls it a NEW BIRTH. We have all been born once as men—but we must see to it we are born again as true Christians. We have been born once of the seed of Adam—woe to us if we are not born the second time of the seed of God! We have been born of the flesh—we must also be born of the Spirit. We are born earthly—we must also be born heavenly. We are born corruptible—we must also be born incorruptible. Our natural birth is as necessary to the life of the body—as our spiritual birth is necessary to the life of the soul.

To be born again is, as it were, to enter upon a new existence, to have a new mind and a new heart, new views, new principles, new tastes, new affections, new likings and new dislikings, new fears, new joys, new sorrows, new love to things once hated, new hatred to things once loved, new thoughts of God and ourselves and the world and the life to come, and the means whereby that life is attained. And it is indeed a true saying that he who has gone through it is a new man, a new creature, for old things are passed away—behold, he can say, all things are become new! It is not so much that our natural powers and faculties are taken away and destroyed; I would rather say that they receive an utterly new bias and direction. It is not that the old metal is cast aside—but it is melted down and refined and remolded, and has a new stamp impressed upon it, and thus, so to speak, becomes a new coin.

This is no external change, like that of Herod, who did many things and then stopped—or of Ahab, who humbled himself and went in sack-cloth and walked softly; nor is it a change which can neither be seen nor felt. It is not merely a new name and a new notion—but the implanting of a new principle which will surely bear good fruit. It is opening the eyes of the blind and unstopping the ears of the deaf; it is loosing the tongue of the dumb, and giving hands and feet to the maimed and lame—for he who is born again no longer allows his members to be instruments and servants of unrighteousness—but he gives them unto God, and then only are they properly employed.

To be born again is to become a member of a new family by adoption, even the family of God; it is to feel that God is indeed our Father, and that we are made the very sons and daughters of the Almighty; it is to become the citizen of a new state, to cast aside the bondage of Satan and live as free men in the glorious liberty of Christ's kingdom, giving our King the tribute of our best affection, and believing that He will keep us from all evil. To be born again is a spiritual resurrection, a faint likeness indeed of the great change at last—but still a likeness; for the new birth of a man is a passage from death to life; it is a passage from ignorance of God to a full knowledge of Him, from slavish fear to childlike love, from sleepy carelessness about Him to fervent desire to please Him, from lazy indifference about salvation to burning, earnest zeal; it is a passage from strangeness towards God to heartfelt confidence, from a state of enmity to a state of peace, from worldliness to holiness, from an earthly, sensual, man-pleasing state of mind to the single-eyed mind that is in Christ Jesus. And this it is to be born of the Spirit.

Beloved, time will not allow me to go further with this subject today. I have endeavored to show you generally why we must all be born again, and what the new birth means; and next Sunday, if the Lord wills, I purpose to show you the manner and means by which this new birth usually comes.

It only remains for me now to commend this matter most solemnly to your consciences. Were it a doctrine of only second-rate importance—were it a point a man might leave uncertain and yet be saved, like Church government or election—I would not press it on you so strongly—but it is one of the two great pillars of the gospel. On the one hand stands salvation by free grace for Christ's sake—but on the other stands renewal of the carnal heart by the Spirit. We must be changed as well as forgiven; we must be renewed as well as redeemed.

And I commend this to you all the more because of the times you live in. Men swallow down sermons about Christ's willingness and Christ's power to save, and yet continue in their sins. They seem to forget there must be the Spirit's work within us, as well as Christ's work for us—there must be something written on the table of our hearts. The strong man, Satan, must be cast out of our house, and Jesus must take possession; and we must begin to know the saints' character experimentally on earth—or we shall never be numbered with them in heaven. Christ is indeed a full and sufficient title to heaven—but we must have about us some fitness for that blessed abode.

I will not shrink from telling you that this doctrine cuts every congregation in two; it is the line of separation between the good fish and the bad, the wheat and the tares. There is a natural part in every congregation, and there is a spiritual part; and few indeed are the churches where we should not be constrained to cry, Lord, here are many called—but very few chosen. The kingdom of God is no mere matter of lips and knees and outward service—it must be within a man, seated in the best place of heart; and I will not hesitate to tell you I fear there are many living members of churches who are exceedingly dead professors.

Examine yourselves, then, I pray you, whether you are born again. Have you good solid reasons for thinking that you have put off the old man which is corrupt, and put on the new man which is created after God in holiness? Are you renewed in the spirit of your minds? Are you bringing forth the fruits of the flesh or the fruits of the Spirit? Are you carnally minded or heavenly minded? Are your affections with the world or with God? Are you natural men or are you spiritual men? Oh! but it were no charity in me to keep back this weighty truth; and it will be no wisdom in you to put off and delay considering it.

Are you born again? Without it no salvation! It is not written that you may not—or yet that you will have some difficulty—but it is written that you cannot without it see the kingdom of God. Consider with yourselves how fearful it will be to be shut out; to see God's kingdom afar off, like the rich man in the parable, and a great gulf between; how terrible to go down to the pit from under the very pulpit, well satisfied with your own condition—but still not born again. There are truly many roads to perdition—but none so melancholy as that which is traveled on by professing Christians—by men and women who have light and knowledge and warning and means and opportunity and yet go smiling on as if sermons and holiness were not meant for them—or as if hell was a bed of roses—or as if God was a liar and could not keep His word.

Are you born again? I do not want to fill your heads—but to move your hearts; it is not a matter of course that all who go to church shall be saved; churches and ministers are meant to rouse you to self-inquiry, to awaken you to a sense of your condition; and next to that grand question, "Have you taken Christ for your Savior?" there comes the second point, "Are you born again?"

Beloved, if you love life, search and see what is your condition. What though you find no tokens for good: better a thousand times to know it now and live, than to know it too late and die eternally!

Praised be God, it is a doctrine bound round with gracious promises: no heart so hard but the Holy Spirit can move it; many a one could set his seal to that, and tell you that he was darkness, darkness that could be felt—but is now light in the Lord. Many of the Corinthians were bad as the worst among you—but they were washed, they were sanctified, they were justified, in the name of the Lord Jesus and by the Spirit of our God. Many of the Ephesians were as completely dead in sins as any of you—but God quickened them, and raised them up, and created them anew unto good works. Examine yourselves and draw near to God with prayer, and He shall draw near to you—but if you ask not, you shall not have.

As for me, I make my supplication unto God, who can make all things new, that His Spirit may touch your hearts with a deep sense of this truth, for without it my preaching is vain; that there may be a mighty shaking and revival among the dry bones; that you may never rest until you are indeed new men and can say, Verily we *were* dead but we are now alive, we *were* lost but we are now found.

Without this new birth, no man or woman can be saved! You may remember I began to speak of it last Sunday morning, and I endeavored to establish in your minds two main points, which it may be well to recall to your recollection now. First, then, I showed you **the reason WHY this new birth is so absolutely necessary to salvation.** It is because of our sinful hearts, our inbred corruption. We are born from the very first with a disposition towards that which is bad; we have no natural readiness to serve God—it is all against the grain; we have no natural insight into the excellence of Christ's spiritual kingdom, no natural love towards His holy laws or desire to obey them, no natural fitness for heaven; an unrenewed man would be miserable in the company of Jesus and the saints. In short, I said, it is not enough that we are born of the flesh once, natural men; we need to be born the second time of God and become spiritual men—or else we shall never taste eternal life.

I then reminded you of the awful carelessness and indifference and deadness and lukewarmness and coldness and slothfulness about religion which does so widely prevail; and I observed that people were always ingenious in framing reasons and making excuses for their own particular neglect of God, always supposing they had some special difficulty to contend with, which no one else had—business—or poverty, trouble—or family—or lack of time—or lack of learning, and the like—always imagining if these difficulties were taken out of the way, that they would be such good Christians; and I then told you that the root of all these difficulties is the natural old heart; and the thing needed is not leisure and ease and money and learning—but a new heart and a new principle within.

Secondly, I went on to set before you **the nature and character of this new birth**. I showed that it was a change not outward only—but inward; not in name only—but in spirit and in truth. It is a change so thorough, so searching, so radical, so complete, that he who has gone through it may be called born again, for he is to all intents and purposes a new man! He was darkness—but he is now light; he was blind—but he can now see; he was sleeping—but he is now awake; he was dead—but he now lives; he was earthly-minded—but he is now heavenly-minded; he was carnal—but he is now spiritual; he was worldly—but he is now godly; he once loved corruptible things best—but he now loves incorruptible things best; he did set his chief affections on that which is mortal—he now sets his heart on that which is immortal.

Lastly, I pressed upon you all **the immense, the surpassing importance of this doctrine**, and I do so now again. I urged you, everyone, to remember—and I repeat it now—it shall avail us nothing that Christ Jesus has brought in righteousness for us, if there be not also the work of the Holy Spirit within us; that it shall profit us nothing to say we are redeemed, if there is not also good evidence that we have been indeed renewed.

I shall now go on, according to my promise, to set before you the first great cause of this new birth, and the means and the manner in which it comes; and I once more pray God that the subject may not be carelessly put aside—but thought over and made useful to all your souls.

I. The first great cause of this new birth. This new birth, then, this great spiritual change—whence does it comes—and how does it begin? Can any man give it to himself when he pleases? Can any change his own heart? No! the thing is impossible. We can no more quicken and impart life to our souls than we can to our bodies; we can no more rise and become new men in our own strength than wash away sins by our own performances. It is impossible! The natural man is as helpless as Lazarus was when he lay still and cold and motionless in the tomb. We may remove the stone, as it were, and expose the sad work of death—but we can do no more. There must be a power far mightier than any power of earth in exercise before the natural man can awake and arise and come forth as a new creature. And to do all this is the special office of the Spirit of Christ, the Holy Spirit, whom Jesus promised to send. It is He who quickens; it is He who gives life. The Spirit alone can make the seed we scatter bear fruit; the Spirit alone can lay the first foundation of that holy kingdom, which we want to see established in your hearts. It is the Spirit who must move over these waste and barren souls before they can become the garden of the Lord. It is the Spirit who must open the darkened windows of our conscience before the true light can shine in upon those chambers within us. And so, he who is born again is born, not of blood, nor of the will of the flesh, nor of the will of man—but of God; for the Spirit is very God.

Beloved, this is a very humbling and solemn truth. The conversion of a sinner can never be that light, off-hand affair that some do seem to think about it. This great change which must come over us can never be a thing so entirely within our reach and grasp that we may put off the old Adam like a cloak, and put on the new man, just when and where we please. Oh—but it is a work that cannot possibly be done without the hand of God! The same Power which first created heaven and earth, and called the fair world around us into being—the same Power alone can create in us new hearts, and renew in us right minds—the same Power alone can convert the natural man into the spiritual.

Yes! you may dream of death-bed repentance, and say, By-and-by we will turn and become Christians—but you know not what you are saying: the softening of the hard heart, and the entrance upon new ways, and the taking up of new principles, is no such easy matter as you seem to imagine—it is work that can only be begun by divine power—and who shall say, that you may not put it off too long?

It is not the plainest and clearest preaching, however lovely it may sound, which can cause men to be born again. Paul may plant and Apollos may water—but the Spirit alone can give the increase! We may raise up congregations fair and formal, and sinews and flesh and skin may cover the dry bones, but they are no better than dead—until the Spirit breathes upon them. Not all the wisdom of Solomon, not all the faith of Abraham, not all the prophecies of Isaiah, not all the eloquence of Apostles, could avail to convert one single soul—without the operation of the Holy Spirit. "Not by might, nor by power—but by my Spirit, says the Lord almighty." And therefore I call this a solemn truth. I know the Spirit is promised to all who ask—but I tremble lest men should loiter and put off their souls' concerns so long, that the Spirit may be grieved—and leave them in their sins.

And still, beloved, solemn as this truth may be to sinners, it is full of consolation to believers; it is full of sweet and unspeakable comfort to all who feel in themselves the holy workings of a new and spiritual nature. These can say with rejoicing, "It is not our right hand nor our arm which has brought us on the way towards Zion; the Lord Himself was on our side; it was He who raised us from the death of sin to the life of righteousness, and surely He will never let us go. Once we were sleeping and dead in trespasses—but the Spirit awakened us and opened our eyes. We caught a sight of the punishment prepared for the ungodly; we heard a voice saying, 'Come unto Me, and I will give you rest,' and we could sleep no longer. And surely we may hope that He, who graciously began the work of grace, will also carry it forward; He laid the foundation, and He will not let it decay; He began, and He will bring His handiwork to perfection."

So much for the great Cause and Giver of the New Birth—the Holy Spirit.

II. The means through which the new birth is ordinarily conveyed, and comes, and the different ways and manners in which it generally shows itself and produces its wonderful effects.

Now, with respect to the means which the Holy Spirit does ordinarily use, I would not have you for one minute suppose that I wish to limit or set bounds to the Holy One of Israel. I do not for an instant deny that some have been born again without any outward visible machinery having been used—by a sort of secret impulse which cannot be well explained—but I do say that, generally speaking, the Holy Spirit, in giving to a man that blessed thing the new birth, is pleased to work upon his heart more or less by means which our eyes can see and which our minds can understand.

I would not, then, have you ignorant that a man is seldom born again of the Spirit, without *the **preaching of the Gospel*** having something to do in the change. This is a special instrument for turning men from darkness to light, and many a one can testify that it was through sermons he was first touched, and brought to the knowledge of the truth. It was Peter's preaching which first touched the men of Jerusalem after our Lord's death, insomuch that they were pricked to the heart and said, "Men and brethren, what shall we do?" It was the command which

Jesus gave to the apostles before his ascension, they were "to preach unto the people and to testify." It was a cause of joy to Paul, that Christ was preached at Rome: "I therein rejoice," he says, "and will rejoice." It was his own declaration about himself, "Christ Jesus sent me not to baptize—but to preach the Gospel." No means is so blessed in all the experience of Christ's Church as the plain preaching of the Gospel; no sign so sure of decay and rottenness in a Church as the neglect of preaching; for there is no ordinance in which the Holy Spirit is so particularly present, none by which sinners are so often converted and brought back to God. Faith comes by hearing; and how shall men believe—unless they hear? Therefore it is that we press upon you so continually to be diligent in hearing Christ preached; for none are so unlikely to be born again as those who will not listen to the truth.

And seldom too is a man born of the Spirit without the **Bible** having something to do in the process. The Bible was written by men who spoke as they were moved by the Holy Spirit, and he who reads it seriously and attentively—or hears it read, is seeking acquaintance with God in God's own way. You would find few indeed among the Lord's true people who would not tell you that the starting-point in their spiritual life was some saying or doctrine in Scripture; some part or portion, pressed home upon their consciences by an unseen, secret power, was among the first things which stirred them up to think and examine their ways; some plain declaration flashed across their minds and made them say, "If this be true I shall certainly be lost." Therefore it is we tell you over and over again, Search the Scriptures, search the Scriptures; they are the sword of the Spirit, they are the weapon by which the devil is often driven out; and he who leaves his Bible unread does plainly not wish to be born again.

Once more. Never are men born of the Spirit without **Prayer**. I believe there would not be found a single case of a person who had been

quickened and made a new creature without God having been entreated
of and inquired of before. Either he has prayed for himself—or some
one has prayed for him: so Stephen died praying for his murderers, and
by-and-by Saul was converted. The Lord loves to be sought after by His
guilty creatures; and they who will not ask for the Holy Spirit to come
down upon them, have no right to expect in themselves any real change.

Such, then, beloved, are the means through which this new birth is
generally given. I say generally, because it is not for me to set bounds to
the operations of God; I know men may be startled by sicknesses and
accidents and the like—but still I repeat that preaching, the Bible and
prayer are the channels through which the Spirit *ordinarily* works. And
I say further that in all my life and reading I never heard of a man who
diligently, humbly, heartily and earnestly made use of these means, who
did not sooner or later find within himself new habits and principles. I
never heard of a man steadily persevering in their use, who did not sooner
or later feel that sin and he must part company—who did not, in short,
become a real child of God, a new creature.

III. So much for the means through which the Spirit generally conveys
this new birth. There is yet one point to be considered this morning;
and that is **the *particular manner* in which this mighty spiritual
change does first touch a person and begin.**

Now, on this point I remark, there are great diversities of operations;
there is a vast variety in the methods by which the Spirit works, and
hence it is that we can never say He is tied down to show himself in one
particular way; we must never condemn a person and tell him he is a
graceless unconverted sinner because his experience may happen to differ
widely from our own.

I would have you note, then, there is great diversity in the **time** and
age at which this change begins. Some few have the grace of God in

them when **very young**; they cannot so much as remember the time when they were without a deep sense of their natural corruption and a lively faith in Christ, and an earnest desire and endeavor to live close to God: such were Isaac and Samuel and Josiah and Jeremiah, and John the Baptist and Timothy. Blessed and happy are these souls; their memories are not saddened by the recollection of years wasted in carelessness and sin; their imaginations are not defiled and stained with the remembrance of youthful wickedness.

But again. Many, perhaps the greater part of true Christians in our day, are never born of the Spirit until they come to age and have reached years of **maturity**. These were once walking after the course of this world, perhaps serving divers lusts and pleasures, perhaps decent outwardly and yet only regarding religion as a thing for Sundays, not as a concern of the hearts. But by some means or other God stops them in their career and turns their hearts back again, and they take up the cross. And bitter indeed is their repentance, and great is their wonder that they could have lived so long in such a fashion, and warm is the love they feel towards Him who has so graciously forgiven them all iniquity.

Once more. Some few, some very few, are first brought unto God and born again in the advance and in **old age**. Oh! but it is fearful to see how few. There are not many who ever arrive at what is called old age; and of these I believe a very insignificant part indeed are ever brought to a saving change. And little wonder if we consider how deeply rooted a thing is habit, how hard it is for those who are accustomed to do evil, to learn to do good. O brethren beloved, youth is the time to seek the Lord! I know that with God nothing is impossible; I know that He can touch the rock that has long been unmoved, if He pleases, and make the water flow—but still we very seldom hear of old men or women being converted: grey hairs are the time for burning the oil of grace and not for buying it, and therefore I say, pray you that your flight be not in the winter of life.

IV. The next thing I would have you note is **the *great diversity in the ways*** **by which the Spirit, so to speak, does strike the first blow in producing this new birth.**

Some are awakened suddenly, **by mighty providences and interpositions of God**; they despise other warnings, and then the Lord comes in and violently shakes them out of sleep, and plucks them like brands from the burning. And this is often done by unexpected mercies—by extraordinary afflictions and troubles, by sicknesses, by accidents, by placing a man in some great danger and peril; and thousands, I am certain, will tell us in heaven, "It is good for us that we were tried and distressed; 'before I was afflicted I went astray—but now have I kept Your word.'" This was the case with Paul: he was struck to the earth blinded, while going to Damascus to persecute, and he rose up a humbled and a wiser man. This was the case with Jonah: when he fled from the Lord's command, he was awakened by a storm while sleeping on board the ship. This was the case with Manasseh, king of Judah: he was taken prisoner and laid in chains at Babylon, and in his affliction he sought the Lord. This was the case with the jailer at Philippi: he was roused by the earthquake, and came and fell down saying, What shall I do to be saved?" This is the case spoken of by Elihu in the thirty-third chapter of Job. And here is the reason why we ought to feel so anxious about a man, when God has laid His hand upon him and afflicted him. I always feel about such a person, "There is one whom the Lord is trying to convert: will it or will it not be all in vain?"

Again. Some are awakened **suddenly, by very little and trifling things**. God often raises up Christ's kingdom in a man's heart by a seed so small and insignificant, that all who see it are obliged to confess, "This is the Lord's doing, and it is marvelous in our eyes." A single text of Scripture sometimes; a few lines in a book taken up by accident; a chance expression or word dropped in conversation, and never perhaps meant by him who spoke it to do so much: each of these seeming trifles has been known to pierce men's hearts like an arrow, after sermons and ordinances have been used without appearing to avail. I have heard of one who could trace up the beginning of his conversion to the saying of a perfect stranger: he was profanely asking God to damn his soul, when the stranger stopped him and said it were better to pray that it might be blessed than damned; and that little word found its way to his heart. Oh, how careful should we be over our lips! Who knows what good might be done if we only strove more to speak a word in season?

Once more. Some are born of the Spirit **gradually and insensibly**. They hardly know at the period what is going on within them; they can hardly recollect any particular circumstances attending their conversion—or fix any particular time—but they do know this, that somehow or other they have gone through a great change, they do know that once they were careless about religion, and now they hold it chief in their affections: once they were blind and now they see. This seems to have been the case with Lydia at Philippi; the Lord gently opened her heart, so that she attended to the things spoken by Paul. This is what Elijah saw in the wilderness; there was the whirlwind and the earthquake and the fire, and after all there was something else—a still small voice. And here is one reason why we sometimes hope and trust that many among the hearers in our congregations may still prove children of God. We try to think that some of you feel more than you seem to do, and that the time is near when you will indeed come out and be separate, and not be ashamed to confess Christ before men.

There is one more diversity I would very shortly notice. Remember there is **diversity in the feelings which the Spirit first excites**: each feeling is moved sooner or later—but they are not moved always in the same order. The new birth shows itself in some by causing exceeding **fear**—they are filled with a strong sense of God's holiness, and they tremble because they have broken His law continually. Others begin with **sorrow**—they can never mourn enough over their past wickedness and ingratitude. Others begin with **love**—they are full of affection towards Him who died for them, and no sacrifice seems too great to make for His sake. But all these works one and the same Spirit—in this man He touches one string, and in that another—but sooner or later all are blended in harmony together, and when the new creation has fully taken place, fear and sorrow and love may all be found at once.

Beloved, time will not allow me to go further with this subject today. I have endeavored to show you this morning who is the Worker, the CAUSE of the new birth: it is not man—but God the Holy Spirit. What are the MEANS through which He generally conveys it: preaching, the Bible, and prayer. And lastly I have shown you there are many DIVER-SITIES in His operations: with some He begins when very young, with some in full years, with some few in old age. On some He comes down suddenly and on some gradually, in some He first moves one sort of feelings and in some another—but whatever be His operation, without the Spirit none can be born again.

And now, in CONCLUSION, tell me not that you mean to wait lazily and idly, and if the Lord gives you this blessed change—that is well; and if not—that you cannot help it. God does not deal with you as if you were machines or stones; He deals with you as those who can read and hear and pray, and this is the way in which He would have you wait upon Him.

Never was doctrine so surrounded with **promises and encourage-ments** and invitations as this. Hear what Jeremiah says: "I will put my law in their inward parts, and write it in their hearts; and will be their God, and they shall be my people." Again: "They shall be my people, and I will be their God: and I will give them one heart, and one way, that they may fear me forever." Then what Ezekiel says: "A new heart also will I give you, and a new spirit will I put within you: and I will take away the stony heart out of your flesh, and I will give you an heart of flesh. And I will put my Spirit within you, and cause you to walk in my statutes." Then lastly what the Lord Jesus says: "Ask, and you shall receive; seek, and you shall find: everyone that asks receives. Your Heavenly Father shall give the Holy Spirit to those who ask Him." And this is what we want you to do: until you pray for yourselves in earnest, we know there will be little good done; and if any prayerless man shall say in the day of judgment "I could not come to Christ," the answer will be, "You did not try."

Then quench not the Spirit, grieve not the Spirit, resist not the Spirit; His grace has been purchased for you: strive and labor and pray that you may indeed receive it. And then God has covenanted and engaged that He shall come down like rain on the dry ground—like water to wash away your soul's defilement, like fire to burn away the dross and filth of sin, and the hardest heart among you shall become soft and willing as a weaned child.

We have reached the last point in our inquiry about the new Birth—I mean the **marks** and **evidences** by which it may be known—the marks by which a man may find out whether he has himself been born again or not. To set before you the character of those who are indeed new creatures—to warn you against certain common mistakes respecting this doctrine—to wind up the whole subject by appealing to your consciences—this is the work which I propose to take in hand this morning.

Now this point may be last in order—but it certainly is not least in importance. It is the touchstone of our condition; it decides whether we

are natural men or spiritual men; whether we are yet dead in trespasses—or have been quickened and brought to see the kingdom of God.

Many there are who take it for granted they have been born
again—they do not exactly know why—but it is a sort of thing they never
doubted. Others there are who despise all such sifting inquiry—they are
sure they are in the right way, they are confident they shall be saved, and
as for marks, it is low and legal to talk about them, it is bringing men
into bondage. But, beloved, whatever men may say, you may be certain
Christ's people are a peculiar people, not only peculiar in their talk—but
peculiar in their life and conduct, and they may be distinguished from
the unconverted around them; you may be certain there are stamps and
marks and characters about God's handiwork by which it may always be
known; and he who has got no evidences to show—well well suspect that
he is not in the right way.

Now, about these marks I can of course only speak very shortly and
very generally, for time will not allow me to do more—but I would first
say one word by way of caution. Remember, then, I would not have
you suppose that all children of God do feel alike—or that these marks
should be equally strong and plain in every case. The work of grace on
man's heart is gradual: first the blade, then the ear, then the full corn
in the ear. It is like leaven: the whole lump is not leavened at once. It
is as in the birth of an infant into the world: first it feels, then moves
and cries, and sees and hears and knows, and thinks and loves, and walks
and talks and acts for itself. Each of these things comes gradually, and in
order—but we do not wait for all before we say this is a living soul. And
just so is everyone that is born of the Spirit. He may not, at first, find in
himself all the marks of God—but he has the seed of them all about him;
and some he knows by experience, and all, in the course of time, shall be
known distinctly.

But this at least you may be sure of: wherever there is no fruit of the Spirit, there is no work of the Spirit; and if any man has not the Spirit of Christ, he is none of His. O that this question might stir up everyone of you to search and try his ways! God is not a man that he should lie; He would not have given you the Bible if you could be saved without it; and here is a doctrine on which eternal life depends: "No salvation without the new birth."

I. First, then, and foremost, I would have you write down in your memories a mark which John mentions in his first epistle: "Whoever makes a **practice of sinning** is of the devil, for the devil has been sinning from the beginning. The reason the Son of God appeared was to destroy the works of the devil. **No one born of God makes a practice of sinning,** for God's seed abides in him, and he cannot keep on sinning because he has been born of God. By this it is evident who are the children of God, and who are the children of the devil: whoever does not **practice righteousness** is not of God, nor is the one who does not love his brother." (1 John 3:8-10)

Observe, I would not for one minute have you suppose that God's children are perfect, and without spot or stain or defilement in themselves. Do not go away and say I told you they were pure as angels and never made a slip or stumble. The same John in the same Epistle declares: "If we say that we have no sin, we deceive ourselves, and the truth is not in us. . . . If we say that we have not sinned, we make Him a liar, and His word is not in us."

But I do say that in the matter of breaking God's commandments, everyone that is born again is quite a new man. He no longer takes a light and cool and easy view of sin; he no longer judges of it with the world's judgment; he no longer thinks a little swearing—or a little Sabbath-breaking—or a little fornication—or a little drinking—or a little covetousness, small and trifling matters—but he looks on every sort of sin against God or man as exceeding abominable and damnable in the Lord's sight, and, as far as in him lies, he hates it and abhors it, and desires to be rid of it root and branch, with his whole heart and mind and soul and strength.

He who is born again has had the eyes of his understanding opened, and the Ten Commandments appear to him in an entirely new light. He feels amazed that he could have lived so long careless and indifferent about transgressions, and he looks back on the days gone by with shame and sorrow and grief. As for his daily conduct, he allows himself in no known sin; he makes no compromise with his old habits and his old principles; he gives them up unsparingly, though it cost him pain, though the world think him over-precise and a fool—but he is a new man, and will have nothing more to do with the accursed thing—sin. I do not say but that he comes short, and finds his old nature continually opposing him—and this, too, when no eye can see it but his own—but then he mourns and repents bitterly over his own weakness. And this at least he has about him: he is at war, in reality, with the devil and all his works, and strives constantly to be free.

And do you call that no change? Look abroad on this world, this evil-doing world: mark how little men generally think about sin; how seldom they judge of it as the Bible does; how easy they suppose the way to heaven—and judge you whether this mark be not exceeding rare. But for all this God will not be mocked, and men may rest assured that until they are convinced of the awful guilt and the awful power and the awful consequences of sin, and, being convinced, flee from it and give it up, they are most certainly not born again.

II. The second mark I would have you note is "**faith in Christ**," and here again I speak in the words of John in his first epistle: "Whoever believes that Jesus is the Christ, is born of God." I do not mean by this a general vague sort of belief that Jesus Christ once lived on earth and died—a sort of faith which the very devils possess. I mean, rather, that feeling which comes over a man when he is really convinced of his own guilt and unworthiness, and sees that Christ alone can be his Savior; when he becomes convinced he is in a way to be lost, and must have some righteousness better than his own, and joyfully embraces that righteousness which Jesus holds out to all who will believe. He who has got this saving faith discovers a fitness and suitableness and comfort in the doctrine of Christ crucified for sinners which once he never knew; he is no longer ashamed to confess himself by nature poor and blind and naked, and to take Christ for his only hope of salvation.

Before a man is born of the Spirit there seems no particular loveliness about the Redeemer—but after that blessed change has taken place, He appears the very chief in ten thousand. There is no honor so great but Jesus is worthy of it. There is no love so strong but on Jesus it is well bestowed. There is no spiritual necessity so great but Jesus can relieve it. There is no sin so black but Jesus' blood can wash it away. Before the new birth a man can bow at Christ's name, and sometimes wonder at Christ's miracles—but that is all. Once born again, a man sees a fullness and a completeness and a sufficiency in Christ of things necessary to salvation, so that he feels as if he could never think upon Him enough. To cast the burden of sin on Jesus, to glory in the cross on which He died, to keep continually in sight His blood, His righteousness, His intercession, His mediation; to go continually to Him for peace and forgiveness, to rest entirely on Him for full and free salvation; to make Jesus, in short, all in all in their hopes of heaven—this is the most notable mark of all true children of God—they live by faith in Christ, in Christ their happiness is bound up.

It is the spiritual law of God which brings them to this: time was when they were ready to think well of themselves; the law strips off their miserable garments of self-righteousness, exposes their exceeding guilt and rottenness, cuts down to the ground their fancied notions of justification by their own works, and so leads them to Christ as their only wisdom and redemption; and then, when they have laid hold on Christ and taken Him for their Savior, they begin to find that rest which before they had sought in vain.

Such are two first marks of the Spirit's work—a deep conviction of sin and forsaking of it. And a lively faith in Christ crucified as the only hope of forgiveness. These are marks which the world perhaps may not see—but marks without which no man or woman was ever yet made a new creature. These are the two foundations of the Christian's character, the pillars, as it were, of the kingdom of God; they are hidden roots which others can only judge of by the fruit—but they who have them do generally know it, and can feel the witness in themselves.

III. The third mark of the new birth is "**holiness**." What says the apostle John again? "You know that everyone who practices righteousness is born of him." (1 John 2:29) "And everyone who thus hopes in Him purifies himself as He is pure." (1 John 3:3)

The true children of God delight in making the law their rule of life; it dwells in their minds, and is written upon their hearts, and it is their food and drink to do their Father's will. They know nothing of that spirit of bondage which false Christians complain of; it is their pleasure to glorify God with their bodies and souls, which are His; they hunger and thirst after tempers and dispositions like their Lord's. They do not rest content with sleepy wishing and hoping—but they strive to be holy in their whole life—in thought, in word, and in deed; it is their daily heart's prayer, "Lord what will You have us to do?" and it is their daily grief and lamentation that they come so short and are such unprofitable servants. Beloved, remember where there is no holiness of life there cannot be much work of the Holy Spirit.

IV. The fourth mark of the new birth is **spiritual-mindedness**. We learn this from Paul's words to the Colossians: "If then you were raised together with Christ, seek the things that are above, where Christ is, seated on the right hand of God. Set your mind on the things that are above, not on the things that are on the earth. For you died, and your life is hidden with Christ in God." (Colossians 3:1-3)

He who is born again thinks first about the things which are eternal; he no longer gives up the best of his heart to this perishable world's concerns. He looks on earth as a place of pilgrimage, he looks on heaven as his home. And even as a child remembers with delight its absent parents, and hopes to be one day with them, so does the Christian think of his God and long for that day when he shall stand in His presence and go no more out. He cares not for the pleasures and amusements of the world around him. He minds not the things of the flesh—but the things of the Spirit. He feels that he has a house not made with hands eternal in the heavens, and he earnestly desires to be there. "Lord," he says, "whom have I in heaven but You? and there is nothing on earth that I desire beside You."

V. The fifth mark of the new birth is victory over the world. Hear what John says: "Whoever is born of God **overcomes the world**: and this is the victory that overcomes the world, even our faith."

What is the natural man? A wretched slave to the opinion of this world. What the world says is right he follows and approves; what the world says is wrong he renounces and condemns also. How shall I do what my neighbors do not do? What will men say of me if I become more strict than they? This is the natural man's argument. But from all this, he who is born again is free. He no longer is led by the praise or the blame, the laughter or the frown, of the world. He no longer thinks that the sort of religion which everybody about him professes must necessarily be right. He no longer considers "What will the world say?" but "What does God command?" Oh, it is a glorious change when a man thinks nothing of the difficulty of confessing Christ before men, in the hope that Christ will confess him and own him before the holy angels! The 'fear of the world' is a terrible snare; with many thousands it far outweighs the fear of God. There are men who would care more for the laughter of a company of friends than they would for the testimony of half the Bible. From all this the spiritual man is free. **He is no longer like a dead fish floating with the stream of earthly opinion**; he is ever pressing upwards, looking unto Jesus in spite of all opposition He has overcome the world.

VI. The sixth mark of the new birth is "**meekness**." This is what David meant when he said, in Psalm 131: "My soul is even as a weaned child." This is what our Lord has in view when He tells us we "must be converted and become as little children."

Pride is the besetting sin of all natural men, and it comes out in a hundred different ways. It was pride by which the angels fell and became devils. It is pride which brings many a sinner to the pit—he knows he is in the wrong about religion—but he is too proud to bend his neck and act up to what he knows. It is pride which may always be seen about false professors: they are always saying—We are the men, and we are alone in the right, and ours is the sure way to heaven; and by-and-by they fall and go to their own place and are heard no more of. But he who is born again is clothed with humility; he has a very child-like and contrite and broken spirit; he has a deep sense of his own weakness and sinfulness, and great fear of a fall. You never hear him professing confidence in himself and boasting of his own attainments—he is far more ready to doubt about his own salvation altogether and call himself "chief of sinners." He has no time to find fault with others—or be a busybody about his neighbors. It is enough for him to keep up the conflict with his own deceitful heart, the old Adam within. No enemy so bitter to him as his own inbred corruption.

Whenever I see a man passing his time in picking holes in other Churches, and talking about everyone's soul except his own, I always feel in my own mind, "There is no work of the Spirit there." And it is just this humility and sense of weakness which makes God's children men of prayer. They feel their own needs and their danger, and they are constrained to go continually with supplication to Him who has given them the Spirit of adoption, crying, Abba Father, help us and deliver us from evil.

VII. The seventh mark of the new birth is a **great delight in all means of grace**. This is what Peter speaks of in his first Epistle: "As new-born babes, desire the sincere milk of the word, that you may grow." This was the mind of David when he said, "A day in Your courts is better than a thousand: I had rather be a doorkeeper in the house of my God, than to dwell in the tents of wickedness."

And oh, what a difference there is between nature and grace in this matter! The natural man has often a form of godliness: he does not neglect the ordinances of religion—but somehow or other the weather—or his health—or the distance, contrives to be a great hindrance to him, and far too often it happens that the hours he spends in church or over his Bible are the dullest in his life.

But when a man is born again, he begins to find a reality about means which once he did not feel: the Sabbath no longer seems a dull, wearisome day, in which he knows not how to spend his time decently; he now calls it a delight and a privilege, holy of the Lord and honorable. The difficulties which once kept him from God's house now seem to have vanished away: dinner and weather and the like never detain him at home, and he is no longer glad of an excuse not to go. Sermons appear a thousand times more interesting than they used to do; and he would no more be inattentive or willingly go to sleep under them, than a prisoner would upon his trial. And, above all, the Bible looks to him like a new book. Time was when it was very dry reading to his mind—perhaps it lay in a corner dusty and seldom read—but now it is searched and examined as the very bread of life; many are the texts and passages which seem just written for his own case; and many are the days that he feels disposed to say with David, "The law of Your mouth is better to me than thousands of gold and silver."

VIII. The eighth and last mark of the new birth is "**love towards others.**" "Beloved, let us love one another, for love is of God; and everyone who loves is born of God, and knows God. He who doesn't love doesn't know God, for God is love." (1 John 4:7-8)

He who is born of the Spirit loves his neighbor as himself; he knows nothing of the selfishness and uncharitableness and ill-nature of this world. He loves his neighbor's **property** as his own; he would not injure it, nor stand by and see it injured. He loves his neighbor's **person** as his own, and he would count no trouble ill bestowed if he could help or assist him. He loves his neighbor's **character** as his own, and you will not hear him speak a word against it—or allow it to be blackened by falsehoods if he can defend it. He loves his neighbor's **soul** as his own, and he will not allow him to turn his back on God without endeavoring to stop him by saying, "Oh, do not so!" Oh what a happy place would earth be if there was more love! Oh that men would only believe that the gospel secures the greatest comfort in the life that now is, as well as in the life to come!

And such, beloved, are the marks by which the new birth in a man's soul may generally be discovered. I have been obliged to speak of them very concisely, although each one of them deserves a sermon. I commend to your especial attention the two first: conviction and forsaking of sin, and faith in Christ; they are marks on which each must be his own judge. "Have I ever truly repented? Have I really closed with Christ and taken Him for my only Savior and Lord?" Let these questions be uppermost in your mind if you would know whether you are born again or not. The six last marks: holiness, spiritual-mindedness, victory over the world, meekness, delight in means of grace, and love—have this peculiarity about them, that a man's family and neighbors do often see more clearly whether he has them than he does himself—but they all flow out of the two first, and therefore I once more urge the two first on your especial notice.

And now, brethren beloved, in concluding this course of sermons, I desire to speak one word to the consciences of all who have heard them: old or young, rich or poor, careless or thoughtful, you are all equally concerned.

For three Sunday mornings you have heard this new birth set before you—have you ever thought upon your own state and looked within? What of your own hearts? Are you living or dead, natural or spiritual, born again or not? Are your bodies temples of the Holy Spirit? Are your habits and characters the habits and characters of renewed creatures? Oh, search and see what there is within you: the language of the text is plain—no new birth, no kingdom of God!

I know there is nothing popular or agreeable about this doctrine; it strikes at the root of all compromising half-and-half religion, and still it is true. Many would like much to escape the punishment of sin, who will not strive to be free from its power; they wish to be justified but not to be sanctified; they desire much to have God's favor—but they care little for God's image and likeness; their talk is of pardon—but not of purity; they think much about God's willingness to forgive—but little about His warning that we be renewed. But this is leaving out of sight, half the work which Christ died to perform: He died that we might become holy as well as happy, He purchased grace to sanctify as well as grace to redeem; and now forgiveness of sin and change of heart must never be separated. "What God has joined together, let no man presume to put asunder." The foundation of God stands firm: "If any man has not the Spirit of Christ, he does not belong to Him."

Beloved, it is easy work to live unto ourselves and take no trouble about religion; the world approves it, and says we shall probably do well at last—but if ever we are to be saved there is another life, and that too on this side the grave, we must live unto God. It is easy to be natural men—we give no offence, and the devil comforts us by saying, as he did to Eve, "You shall not surely die!" But the devil was a liar from the beginning. So long as we are natural men, we are dead already, and we must rise to newness of life. And what know you of the movements of the Spirit? I ask not so much whether you can say which way He came into your hearts—but I do ask whether you can find any real footsteps or traces or tokens of His presence—for "If any man has not the Spirit of Christ, he does not belong to Him."

Be not deceived and led away by false opinions. Head-knowledge is not the new birth: a man may know all mysteries like Balaam, and think his eyes are opened; or preach and work miracles and be an Apostle like Judas Iscariot, yet never be born again. Church-membership is not the new birth; many do sit in churches and chapels who shall have no seat in Christ's kingdom; they are not Israel who have the circumcision of the flesh outwardly, they are the true Israel who have the circumcision of the heart, which is inward. There were many Jews in the New Testament days who said, "We have Abraham for our father, and we have the temple among us and that is enough," but Jesus showed them that they only are Abraham's children who have the faith of Abraham and do Abraham's works.

And neither is water-baptism the new birth: it is the sign and seal, and when used with faith and prayer we have a right to look also for the baptism of the Holy Spirit—but to say that every man who has been baptized has been born again is contrary to Scripture and plain fact. Was not Simon Magus baptized? Yes—but Peter told him after his baptism that he was in the gall of bitterness and bond of iniquity, his heart not right in the sight of God. "I would not have you ignorant," says Paul to the Corinthians, that all our Fathers were baptized, ... but with many of them God was not well pleased. "Baptism," writes Peter, "does indeed save us"—but what baptism? "not the putting away of the filth of the body, not the washing of water—but the answer of a pure conscience," a conscience made pure by the baptism of the Holy Spirit.

Beloved, let no man lead you astray in this matter; let no man make you believe that a baptized drunkard or fornicator or blasphemer or worldling has been born of the Spirit; he has not the marks of the new birth, and he cannot have been born again; he is living in sin and carelessness, and John has given us his character, "he who practices sin is of the devil." Remember, the outward seal is nothing without the inward writing on the heart. No evidence can be depended on, except a new life and a new character and a new creature; and to say that men who lack biblical evidences are born again, is an unreasonable and unscriptural stretch of charity.

And now, in conclusion, if any one of you has reason to think that he still lacks this one thing needful, I entreat that man not to stifle his convictions or nip them in the bud. Do not go away like Cain and silence the voice of conscience by rushing into the vanities of the world; nor dream, like Felix, that you will have a more convenient season than the present. But remember I tell you this day there are two things which make a death-bed especially uncomfortable: first, purposes and promises not performed; and second, convictions slighted and not improved. And if any of you has satisfactory grounds for thinking that he has really tasted something of that saving and necessary change we have considered, I charge that man not to stand still, not to loiter, not to linger, not to look behind him; I warn him that none are in so dangerous a way as those who have become cool and cold and indifferent after real and warm concern about salvation; I urge him to press forward more and more towards the knowledge of Christ, and to remember it is a special mark of God's children that as they grow in age they grow in grace, and feel their sins more deeply and love their Lord and Savior more sincerely.

Chapter Three

Are You Regenerate?

R eader, I wish to speak to you about Regeneration, or being born again.

The subject is a most important one at any time. Those words of our Lord Jesus Christ to Nicodemus are very solemn, "Unless a man be born again, he cannot see the kingdom of God." (John 3:3.) The world has gone through many changes since those words were spoken. Eighteen hundred years have passed away. Empires and kingdoms have risen and fallen. Great men and wise men have lived, labored, written, and died. But there stands the rule of the Lord Jesus unaltered and unchanged. And there it will stand, until heaven and earth shall pass away—"Unless a man be born again, he cannot see the kingdom of God."

But the subject is one which is doubly important in the present day. Things have happened which have drawn special attention to it. Men's minds are full of it, and men's eyes are fixed on it. Regeneration is discussed in newspapers. Regeneration is talked of in private society. Regeneration is argued about in courts of law. Surely it is a time when every true Christian should examine himself upon the subject, and make sure that his views are sound. It is a time when we should not halt between two opinions. We should try to know what we hold. We should be ready to give a reason for our belief. When the truth is assailed, those who love truth should grasp it more firmly than ever. Oh, for a greater spirit of decision throughout the land! Oh, for a more hearty determination to be always on the Lord's side!

Reader, I invite you to listen to me, while I try to bring this disputed question before you. I feel deeply that I can tell you nothing new. I know I can say nothing which has not been better said by better men than myself. But every additional witness may be of use in a disputed cause. And if I can only throw a little Scripture light on the subject of Regeneration, and make it plain to plain readers of the Bible, I shall thank God, and be abundantly satisfied. What are the opinions of men to you or me? He who judges us is the Lord! One point has to be ascertained, and only one. "What do the Scripture of truth say?"

Now I propose to attempt three things—

I. Firstly, to explain *what Regeneration, or being born again, means.*
II. Secondly, to show the *necessity of Regeneration.*
III. Thirdly, to point out *the marks and evidences of Regeneration.*

If the Lord God shall enable me to make these three points clear to you, I believe I shall have done your soul a great service.

I. Let me then, first of all, explain *what Regeneration, or being born again, means.*

Regeneration means, that change of heart and nature which a man goes through when he becomes a true Christian.

I think there can be no question that there is an immense difference among those who profess and call themselves Christians. Beyond all dispute, there are always two classes in the outward Church—the class of those who are Christians in name and form only, and the class of those who are Christians in deed and in truth. All were not Israel who were called Israel, and all are not Christians who are called Christians. "In the visible Church," says an article of the Church of England, "the evil be ever mingled with the good."

Some, as the Thirty-nine Articles say, are "wicked and void of a lively faith." Others, as another article says, "are made like the image of God's only-begotten Son, Jesus Christ, and walk piously in good works." Some worship God as a mere form—and some in spirit and in truth. Some give their hearts to God—and some give them to the world. Some believe the Bible, and live as if they believed it—others do not. Some feel their sins, and mourn over them—others do not. Some love Christ, trust in Him, and serve Him—others do not. In short, as Scripture says, some walk in the narrow way—some in the broad way; some are the good fish of the Gospel net—some are the bad fish; some are the wheat in Christ's field—some are the tares.

I think no man with his eyes open can fail to see all this, both in the Bible, and in the world around him. Whatever he may think about the subject I am writing of, he cannot possibly deny that this difference exists.

Now what is the explanation of the difference? I answer unhesitating-ly— Regeneration, or being born again. I answer, that true Christians are what they are, because they are Regenerate; and formal Christians are what they are, because they are not Regenerate. The heart of the true Christian has been changed. The heart of the Christian in name only, has not been changed. The change of heart makes the whole difference.

This change of heart is spoken of continually in the Bible, under various emblems and figures—

Ezekiel calls it, "a taking away the stony heart, and giving an heart of flesh;"—"a giving a new heart, and putting within us a new spirit." (Ezek. 11:19; 36:26.)

The apostle John sometimes calls it, being "born of God," sometimes, being "born again," sometimes, being "born of the Spirit." (John 1:13; 3:3-6.)

The apostle Peter, in the Acts, calls it "repenting and being converted." (Acts 3:19.)

The Epistle to the Romans speaks of it as a "being alive from the dead." (Rom. 6:13.)

The second Epistle to the Corinthians calls it "being a new creature—old things have passed away, and all things become new." (2 Cor. 5:17.)

The Epistle to the Ephesians speaks of it as a resurrection together with Christ—"You has He quickened who were dead in trespasses and sins" (Ephes. 2:1); as "a putting off the old man, which is corrupt—being renewed in the spirit of our minds—and putting on the new man, which after God is created in righteousness and true holiness." (Ephes. 4:22, 24.)

The Epistle to the Colossians calls it a "putting off the old man with his deeds, and putting on the new man, which is renewed in knowledge after the image of Him that created him." (Coloss. 3:9, 10.)

The Epistle to Titus calls it, "the washing of Regeneration and renewing of the Holy Spirit." (Titus 3:5.)

The first Epistle of Peter speaks of it as "a being called out of darkness into God's marvelous light." (1 Peter 2:9.) And the second Epistle as "being made partakers of the divine nature." (2 Peter 1:4.)

The first Epistle of John calls it a "passing from death to life." (1 John 3:14.)

All these expressions come to the same thing in the end. They are all the same truths only viewed from different sides. And all have one and the same meaning. They describe a great radical change of heart and nature—a thorough alteration and transformation of the whole inner man—a participation in the resurrection life of Christ—or, to borrow the words of the Church of England Catechism, "a death unto sin and a new birth unto righteousness."

This change of heart in a true Christian is so complete, that no word could be chosen more fitting to express it than that word, "Regeneration," or "new birth." Doubtless it is no outward, bodily alteration—but undoubtedly it is an entire alteration of the inner man. It adds no new faculties to a man's mind—but it certainly gives an entirely new bent and bias to all his old ones. His will is so new, his tastes so new, his opinions so now, his views of sin, the world, the Bible, and Christ so new, that he is to all intents and purposes a new man. The change seems to bring a new being into existence. It may well be called being *born again.*

This change is *not always given to believers at the same time in their lives.* A vast multitude of people it is to be feared, go down to the grave without having been born again at all.

This change of heart *does not always begin in the same way.* With some, like the apostle Paul, and the jailor at Philippi, it is a sudden and violent change, attended with much distress of mind. With others, like Lydia of Thyatira, it is more gentle and gradual—their winter becomes spring almost without their knowing how. With some the change is brought about by the Spirit working through afflictions or providential visitations. With others, and probably the greater number of true Christians, the Word of God, preached or written, is the means of effecting it.*

* "The preaching of the Word is the great means which God has appointed for Regeneration—'faith comes by hearing, and hearing by the Word of God.' (Rom. 10:17.) When God first created man, it is said that 'He breathed into his nostrils the breath of life,' but when God new creates man, He breathes into his ears. This is the Word that raises the dead, calling them out of the grave—this is that Word that opens the eyes of the blind, that turns the heart of the disobedient and rebellious. And though wicked and profane men scoff at preaching, and count all ministers' words, and God's words too—but so much wind, yet they are such wind, believe it, as is able to tear rocks and rend mountains; such winds, as if ever they are saved, must shake and overturn the foundations of all their carnal confidence and presumption. Be exhorted, therefore, more to prize and more to frequent the preaching of the Word."—*Hopkins.* 1670.

This change is one which *can only be known and discerned by its effects*. Its beginnings are a hidden and secret thing. We cannot see them. Our Lord Jesus Christ tells us this most plainly—"The wind blows where it wills, and you hear the sound thereof—but cannot tell whence it comes or where it goes; so is everyone that is born of the Spirit." (John 3:8.) Would you know if you are Regenerate? You must try the question, by examining what you know of the effects of Regeneration. Those effects are always the same. The ways by which true Christians are led, in passing through their great change, are certainly various. But the state of heart and soul into which they are brought at last, is always the same. Ask them what they think of sin, Christ, holiness, the world, the Bible, and prayer, and you will find them all of one mind.

This change is *one which no man can give to himself, nor yet to another.* It would be as reasonable to expect the dead to raise themselves, or to require an artist to give a marble statue life. The sons of God are "born not of blood, nor of the will of the flesh, nor of the will of man—but of God." (John 1:13.) Sometimes the change is ascribed to God the Father—"The God and Father of our Lord Jesus Christ has begotten us again unto a living hope." (1 Peter 1:3.) Sometimes it is ascribed to God the Son—"The Son quickens whom He will." (John 3:21.) "If you know that He is righteous, you know that everyone that does righteousness is born of Him." (1 John 2:29.) Sometimes it is ascribed to the Spirit—and He, in fact, is the great agent by whom it is always effected—"That which is born of the Spirit is Spirit." (John 3:6.) But man has no power to work the change. It is something far, far beyond his reach. "The condition of man after the fall of Adam," says the tenth Article of the Church of England, "is such that he cannot turn and prepare himself by his own natural strength and good works, to faith and calling upon God." No minister on earth can convey grace to any one of his congregation at his discretion. He may preach as truly and faithfully as Paul or Apollos—but God must give the increase. (1 Cor. 3:6.) He may baptize with water in the name of the Trinity—but unless the Holy Spirit accompanies and blesses the ordinance, there is no death unto sin, and no new birth unto righteousness. Jesus alone, the great Head of the Church, can baptize with the Holy Spirit. Blessed and happy are they, who have the inward baptism, as well as the outward.*

---

*"The Scripture teaches, that no more than a child can beget itself, or a dead man quicken himself, or a nonentity create itself; no more can any carnal man regenerate himself, or work true saving grace in his own soul."—*H*

opkins. 1670.

"There are two kinds of baptism, and both necessary—the one interior, which is the cleansing of the heart, the drawing of the Father, the operation of the Holy Spirit—and this baptism is in man when he believes and trusts that Christ is the only method of his salvation."—*Hooper* . 1547.

"It is on all parts gladly confessed, that there may be, in divers cases, life by virtue of inward baptism, where outward is not found."—*Hooper*. 1592.

"There is a baptism of the Spirit as of water."—*Jeremy Taylor*. 1660.

Reader, I lay before you the foregoing account of Regeneration. I say it is that change of heart which is the distinguishing mark of a true Christian man—the invariable companion of a justifying faith in Christ—the inseparable consequence of vital union with him. and the root and beginning of inward sanctification. I ask you to ponder it well before you go any further. It is of the utmost importance that your views should be clear upon this point—*what Regeneration really is.*

I know well that many will not allow that Regeneration is what I have described it to be. They will think the statement I have made, by way of definition, much too strong. Some hold that Regeneration only means admission into a state of ecclesiastical privileges—being made a member of the Church—but does not mean a change of heart. Some tell us that a Regenerate man has a certain power within him which enables him to repent and believe if he thinks fit—but that he still needs a further change in order to make him a true Christian. Some say there is a difference between Regeneration and being born again. Others say there is a difference between being born again and conversion.

To all this I have one simple reply—and that is, *I can find no such Regeneration spoken of anywhere in the Bible*. A Regeneration which only means admission into a state of ecclesiastical privileges may be ancient and primitive, for anything I know. But something more than this is needed. A few plain texts of Scripture are needed; and these texts have yet to be found.

Such a notion of Regeneration is utterly inconsistent with that which John gives us in his first epistle. It renders it necessary to invent the awkward theory that there are two Regenerations, and is thus eminently calculated to confuse the minds of unlearned people, and introduce false doctrine. It is a notion which seems not to answer to the solemnity with which our Lord introduces the subject to Nicodemus. When He said, "Verily, verily, unless a man be born again, he cannot see the kingdom of God," did He only mean, unless a man be admitted to a state of ecclesiastical privilege? Surely He meant more than this. Such a Regeneration a man might have, like Simon Magus, and yet never be saved. Such a Regeneration He might never have, like the penitent thief, and yet see the kingdom of God. Surely He must have meant a change of heart. As to the notion that there is any distinction between being Regenerate and being born again, it is one which will not bear examination. It is the general opinion of all who know Greek, that the two expressions mean one and the same thing.

To me indeed there seems to be much confusion of ideas, and indistinctness of apprehension in men's minds on this simple point—what Regeneration really is—and all arising from not simply adhering to the

Word of God. That a man is admitted into a state of great privilege when he is made a member of a pure Church of Christ, I do not for an instant deny. That he is in a far better and more advantageous position for his soul, than if he did not belong to the Church, I make no question. That a wide door is set open before his soul, which is not set before the poor heathen, I can most clearly see. *But I do not see that the Bible ever calls this Regeneration.* And I cannot find a single text in Scripture which warrants the assumption that it is so. It is very important in theology to distinguish things that differ. Church privileges are one thing. Regeneration is another. I, for one, dare not confound them.

I am quite aware that great and good men have clung to that low view of Regeneration, to which I have adverted.* But when a doctrine of the everlasting Gospel is at stake, I can call no man master. The words of the old philosopher are never to be forgotten—"I love Plato, I love Socrates—but I love truth better than either." I say unhesitatingly, that those who hold the view that there are two Regenerations, can bring forward no plain text in proof of it. I firmly believe that no plain reader of the Bible only, would ever find this view there for himself; and that goes very far to make me suspect it is an idea of man's invention. The only Regeneration that I can see in Scripture is, not a change of *state*—but a change of *heart*. That is the view, I once more assert, which the Church Catechism takes when it speaks of the "death unto sin, and new birth unto righteousness," and on that view I take my stand.

* For instance, Bishop Davenant and Bishop Hopkins frequently speak of "a sacramental Regeneration,' when they are handling the subject of baptism, as a thing entirely distinct from spiritual Regeneration. The general tenor of their writings is to speak of the godly as the regenerate, and the ungodly as the unregenerate. But with every feeling of respect for two such good men, the question yet remains—What

Scripture warrant have we for saying there are two Regenerations? I answer unhesitatingly—We have none at all.

Reader, the doctrine before you is one of vital importance. This is no matter of names, and words, and forms, about which I am writing, and you are reading. It is a thing that you and I must feel and know by experience, each for himself, if we are to be saved. Try, I beseech you, to become acquainted with it. Let not the din and smoke of controversy draw off your attention from your own heart. Is that heart changed? Alas, it is poor work to wrangle, and argue, and dispute about Regeneration, if after all we know nothing about it within.

Reader, Regeneration, or new birth, is the distinguishing mark of every true Christian. Now just consider what I say. *Are you Regenerate, or are you not?*

II. Let me show you, in the second place, *the necessity there is for our being Regenerated, or born again.*

That there is such a necessity is most plain from our Lord Jesus Christ's words in the third chapter of John's Gospel. Nothing can be more clear and positive than His language to Nicodemus—"Unless a man be born again, he cannot see the kingdom of God." "Marvel not that I said unto you, You must be born again." (John 3:7.)

The reason of this necessity is the exceeding sinfulness and corruption of our natural hearts. The words of Paul to the Corinthians are literally accurate—"The natural man receives not the things of the Spirit of God, for they are foolishness unto him." (1 Cor. 2:14.) Just as rivers flow downward, and sparks fly upward, and stones fall to the ground, so does a man's heart naturally incline to what is evil. We love our soul's enemies—we dislike our soul's friends. We call good evil, and we call evil good. We take pleasure in ungodliness, we take no pleasure in Christ. We not only commit sin—but we also love sin. We not only need to be cleansed from the guilt of sin—but we also need to be delivered from its power. The natural tone, bias, and current, of our minds, must be completely altered. The image of God, which sin has blotted out, must be restored. The disorder and confusion which reigns within us must be put down. The first things must no longer be last, and the last first. The Spirit must let in the light on our hearts, put everything in its right place, and create all things new.

It ought always to be remembered that there are two distinct things which the Lord Jesus Christ does for every sinner whom He undertakes to save. He washes him from his sins in His own blood, and gives him a free pardon—*this is his justification*. He puts the Holy Spirit into his heart, and makes him an entire new man—*this is his Regeneration*.

The two things are *both absolutely necessary to salvation*. The change of heart is as necessary as the pardon; and the pardon is as necessary as the change. Without the pardon we have no right or title to heaven. Without the change we would not be fit and ready to enjoy heaven, even if we got there.

The two things are *never separate*. They are never found apart. Every justified man is also a Regenerate man, and every Regenerate man is also a justified man. When the Lord Jesus Christ gives a man remission of sins, He also gives him repentance. When He grants peace with God, He also grants power to become a son of God. There are two great standing maxims of the glorious Gospel, which ought never to be forgotten. One is, "He who believes not shall be damned." (Mark 16:16.) The other is, "If any man has not the Spirit of Christ, he is none of His." (Rom. 8:9.)

Reader, the man who denies the universal necessity of Regeneration, can know very little of the heart's corruption. He is blind indeed who fancies that pardon is all we need in order to get to heaven, and does not see that pardon without a change of heart would be a useless gift. Blessed be God that both are freely offered to us in Christ's Gospel, and that Jesus is able and willing to give the one as well as the other.

Surely you must be aware that the vast majority of people in the world *see nothing, feel nothing, and know nothing in religion as they ought.* How and why is this, is not the present question. I only put it to your conscience—is it not the fact?

Tell them of the **sinfulness** of many things which they are doing continually—and what is generally the reply? "They see no harm."

Tell them of the awful **peril** in which their souls are—of the shortness of time—the nearness of eternity—the uncertainty of life—the reality of judgment. "They feel no danger."

Tell them of their need of a **Savior**—mighty, loving, and divine, and of the impossibility of being saved from hell, except by faith in Him. It all falls flat and dead on their ears. "They see no such great barrier between themselves and heaven."

Tell them of **holiness**, and the high standard of living which the Bible requires. They cannot comprehend the need of such strictness. "They see no use in being so very good."

There are thousands and tens of thousands of such people on every side of us. They will hear these things all their lives. They will even attend the ministry of the most striking preachers, and listen to the most powerful appeals to their consciences. And yet, when you come to visit them on their deathbeds, they are like men and women who never heard these things at all. They know nothing of the leading doctrines of the Gospel by experience. They can render no reason whatever of their own hope.

And why is all this? What is the explanation—what is the cause of such a state of things? It all comes from this—that man naturally has no sense of spiritual things. In vain the sun of righteousness shines before him—the eyes of his soul are blind, and cannot see. In vain the music of Christ's invitations sounds around him—the ears of his soul are deaf and cannot hear it. In vain the wrath of God against sin is set forth—the perceptions of his soul are stopped up—like the sleeping traveler, he does not perceive the coming storm. In vain the bread and water of life are offered to him—his soul is neither hungry for the one, nor thirsty for the other. In vain he is advised to flee to the Great Physician—his soul is unconscious of its disease—why should he go? In vain you put a price into his hand to buy wisdom—the mind of his soul wanders; he is like the lunatic who calls straws a crown, and dust diamonds—he says, "I am rich, and increased with goods, and have need of nothing." Ah, reader, there is nothing so sad as the utter corruption of our nature! There is nothing so painful as the anatomy of a dead soul.

Now what does such a man need? He needs to be born again, and made a new creature. He needs a complete putting off the old man, and a complete putting on the new. We do not live our natural life until we are born into the world; and we do not live our spiritual life until we are born of the Spirit.

But, reader, you must furthermore be aware that the vast majority of people *are utterly unfit to enjoy heaven in their present state.* I lay it before you as a great fact. Is it not so?

Look at the masses of men and women gathered together in our cities and towns, and observe them well. They are all dying creatures—all immortal beings—all going to the judgment seat of Christ—all certain to live forever in heaven or in hell. But where is the slightest evidence that most of them are in the least degree fit and ready for heaven?

Look at the greater part of those who are called Christians, in every part throughout the land. Take any parish you please in town or country. Take that which you know best. What are the tastes and pleasures of the majority of people who live there? What do they like best, when they have a choice? What do they enjoy most, when they can have their own way? Observe the manner in which they spend their Sundays. Mark how little delight they seem to feel in the Bible and prayer. Take notice of the low and earthly notions of pleasure and happiness, which everywhere prevail, among young and old, among rich and poor. Mark well these things, and then think quietly over this question—**"What would these people do in heaven?"**

You and I, it may be said, know little about heaven. Our notions of heaven may be very dim and indistinct. But at all events, I suppose we are agreed in thinking that heaven is a very holy place—that God is there—and Christ is there—and saints and angels are there—that sin is not there in any shape—and that nothing is said, thought, or done, which God does not like. Only let this be granted, and then I think *there can be no doubt the great majority of professing Christians are as little fit for heaven as a bird for swimming beneath the sea, or a fish for living upon dry land.*

And what is it they need in order to make them fit to enjoy heaven? They need to be Regenerated or born again. It is not a little changing and outward amendment they require. It is not merely the putting a restraint on raging passions, and the quieting of unruly affections. All this is not enough. Old age—the lack of opportunity for indulgence—the fear of man, may produce all this. *The tiger is still a tiger, even when he is chained; and the serpent is still a serpent, even when he lies motionless and coiled up.* The alteration needed is far greater and deeper. They must have a new nature put within them. They must be made new creatures. The fountain-head must be purified. The root must be set right. Each one needs a new heart and a new will. The change required is not that of the snake, when he casts his skin and yet remains a reptile still. It is the change of the caterpillar, when he dies and his crawling life ceases—but from his body rises the butterfly—a new animal, with a new nature. All this, and nothing less, is required.

The plain truth is, the vast proportion of professing Christians in the churches have nothing whatever of Christianity, except the name. The reality of Christianity, the graces, the experience, the faith, the hopes, the life, the conflict, the tastes, the hungering and thirsting after right-eousness—all these are things of which they know nothing at all. They need to be converted as truly as any among the heathen to whom Paul preached, and to be turned from idols, and renewed in the spirit of their minds, as really, if not as literally. And one main part of the message which should be continually delivered to the greater portion of every congregation on earth, is this—"You must be born again." I write this down deliberately. I know it will sound dreadful and uncharitable in many ears. But I ask anyone to take the New Testament in his hand and see what it says is Christianity, and compare that with the ways of professing Christians, and then deny the truth of what I have written, if he can.

And now let everyone who reads these pages remember this grand principle of Scriptural religion—**"No salvation without Regenera-tion—no spiritual life without a new birth—no heaven without a new heart."**

Think not for a moment that the subject of this tract is a mere matter of controversy—an empty question for learned men to argue about—but not one that concerns you. Away with such an idea forever! It concerns you deeply. It touches your own eternal interests. It is a thing that you must know for yourself, feel for yourself, and experience for yourself, if you would ever be saved. **No man, woman, or child, will ever enter heaven without having been born again.***

* "Make sure to yourselves this great change. It is no notion that I have now preached unto you. Your natures and your lives must be changed, or, believe it, you will be found at the last day under the wrath of God. For God will not change or alter the Word that is gone out of His mouth. He has said it—Christ, who is the truth and Word of God, has pronounced it—that without the new birth, or Regeneration, no man shall inherit the kingdom of God."—*Hopkins*. 1670.

And think not for one moment that this Regeneration is a change which people may go through after they are dead, though they never went through it while they were alive. Away with such a notion forever! Now or never is the only time to be saved. Now, in this world of toil and labor—of money—getting and business—now you must be prepared for heaven, if you are ever to be prepared at all. Now is the only time to be justified, now the only time to be sanctified, and now the only time to be born again. So sure as the Bible is true, the man who dies without these three things, will only rise again at the last day to be lost forever.

You may be saved, and reach heaven without many things which men reckon of great importance—without riches, without learning, without books, without worldly comforts, without health, without house, without land, without friends—but *without Regeneration you will never be saved at all*. Without your natural birth you would never have lived, and moved on earth; without a new birth you will never live and move in heaven. I bless God that the saints in glory will be a multitude that no man can number. I comfort myself with the thought that, after all, there will be "a great multitude" in heaven. But this I know and am persuaded of from God's Word, that of all who reach heaven, there will not be one single individual who has not been born again.*

* "Regeneration, or the new birth, is of absolute necessity unto eternal life. There is no other change simply necessary—but only this. If you are

poor, you may so continue, and yet be saved. If you are despised, you may
so continue, and yet be saved. If you are unlearned, you may so continue,
and yet be saved. Only one change is necessary. If you are wicked and
ungodly and continued so, Christ, who has the keys of heaven, who shuts
and no man opens, has Himself doomed you, that you shall never enter
into the kingdom of God."—*Hopkins*. 1670.

"Are you born again?" I say to everyone whose eye is upon this page.
Once more I repeat what I have already said, "No salvation without a
new birth."

III. Let me, in the third place, point out *the marks of being*
regenerate, or born again.

It is a most important thing to have clear and distinct views on this part
of the subject we are considering. You have seen what Regeneration is,
and why it is necessary to salvation. The next step is to find out the signs
and evidences by which a man may know whether he is born again or
not—whether his heart has been changed by the Holy Spirit, or whether
his change is yet to come.

Now these signs and evidences are laid down plainly for us in Scripture. God has not left us in ignorance on this point. He foresaw how
some would torture themselves with doubts and questionings, and
would never believe it was well with their souls. He foresaw how others
would take it for granted they were Regenerate who had no right to do
so at all. He has therefore mercifully provided us with a test and gauge
of our spiritual condition, in the First Epistle general of John. There
He has written for our learning, what the Regenerate man is, and what
the Regenerate man does—his ways, his habits, his manner of life, his
faith, his experience. Everyone who wishes to possess the key to a right
understanding of this subject, should thoroughly study this First Epistle
of John.

Reader, I invite your particular attention to these marks and evidences of Regeneration, while I try to set them before you in order. Forget everything else in this volume, if you will—but do not forget this part of it. I might easily mention other evidences besides those I am about to mention. But I will not do so. I would rather confine myself to the First Epistle of John, because of the peculiar explicitness of its statements about the man that is born of God. He that has an ear, let him hear what the beloved Apostle says about the marks of Regeneration.

1. First of all, John says, "No one born of God makes a practice of sinning, for God's seed abides in him, and he cannot keep on sinning because he has been born of God." "We know that everyone who has been born of God does not keep on sinning." (1 John 3:9; 5:18.)

A Regenerate man *does not commit sin as a habit*. He no longer sins with his heart and will, and whole inclination, as an unregenerate man does. There was probably a time when he did not think whether his actions were sinful or not, and never felt grieved after doing evil. There was no quarrel between him and sin—they were friends. Now he hates sin, flees from it, fights against it, counts it his greatest plague, groans under the burden of its presence, mourns when he falls under its influence, and longs to be delivered from it altogether. In one word, sin no longer pleases him, nor is even a matter of indifference—it has become the abominable thing which he hates. He cannot prevent it dwelling within him. "If he said he had no sin, there would be no truth in him" (1 John 1:8)—but he can say that he keenly abhors it, and the great desire of his soul is not to commit sin at all. He cannot prevent bad thoughts arising within him, and shortcomings, omissions, and defects appearing, both in his words and actions. He knows, as James says, that "In many things we offend all." (James 3:2.) But he can say truly, and as in the sight of God, that these things are a daily grief and sorrow to him, and that his whole nature does not consent unto them, as that of the unregenerate man does. Reader, I place this mark before you. What would the Apostle say about you? Are you born of God?*

* "The interpretation of this place that I judge to be the most natural and unforced, is this—'No one born of God makes a practice of sinning;' that is, he does not sin in that malignant manner in which the children of the devil do—he does not make a trade of sin, nor live in the constant and allowed practice of it. There is a great difference between regenerate and unregenerate people in the very sins that they commit. All indeed sin—but a child of God cannot sin—that is, though he does sin, yet he cannot sin after such a manner as wicked and unregenerate men do."—*Hopkins*. 1670.

2. Secondly. John says, "Whoever believes that Jesus is the Christ is born of God." (1 John 5:1.)

A Regenerate man believes that Jesus Christ is the only Savior by whom his soul can be pardoned and redeemed; that He is the divine person appointed and anointed by God the Father for this very purpose, and that beside Him there is no Savior at all. In himself he sees nothing but unworthiness—but in Christ he sees ground for the fullest confidence, and trusting in Him, he believes that his sins are all forgiven and his iniquities all put away. He believes that for the sake of Christ's finished work and death upon the cross, he is reckoned righteous in God's sight, and may look forward to death and judgment without alarm. He may have his doubts and fears. He may sometimes tell you he feels as if he had no faith at all. But ask him whether he is willing to trust in anything instead of Christ, and see what he will say. Ask him whether he will rest his hopes of eternal life on his own goodness, his own amendments, his prayers, his minister, his doings in Church and out of Church, either in whole or in part, and see what he will reply. Ask him whether he will give up Christ, and place his confidence in any other way of salvation. Depend upon it he would say, that though he does feel weak and bad, he would not give up Christ for all the world. Depend upon it—he would say he found a preciousness in Christ, a suitableness to his own soul in Christ, that he found no where else, and that he must cling to Him.

Reader, I place this mark also before you. What would the Apostle say about you? Are you born of God?

3. Thirdly. John says, "Everyone that does righteousness is born of Him." (1 John 2:29.)

The Regenerate man is a *holy man*. He endeavors to live according to God's will, to do the things that please God, to avoid the things that God hates. His aim and desire is to love God with heart and soul, and mind and strength, and to love his neighbor as himself. His wish is to be continually looking to Christ as his example as well as his Savior, and to show himself Christ's friend by doing whatever Christ commands. No doubt he is not perfect. None will tell you that sooner than himself. He groans under the burden of indwelling corruption cleaving to him. He finds an evil principle within him constantly warring against grace, and trying to draw him away from God. But he does not consent to it, though he cannot prevent its presence. In spite of all short-comings, the average bent and bias of his ways is holy—his doings holy—his tastes holy—and his habits holy. In spite of all his swerving and turning aside, like a ship going against a contrary wind, the general course of his life is in one direction—toward God and for God. And though he may sometimes feel so low that he questions whether he is a Christian at all, in his calmer moments he will generally be able to say, with old John Newton, "I am not what I ought to be, I am not what I want to be, I am not what I hope to be in another world—but still I am not what I once used to be, and by the grace of God I am what I am."*

* "Let none conclude that they have no grace, because they have many imperfections in their obedience. Your grace may be very weak and imperfect, and yet you may be truly born again to God, and be a genuine son and heir of heaven."—*Hopkins.* 1670.

Reader, I place this mark also before you. What would the Apostle say about you? Are you born of God?

4. Fourthly. John says, "We know that we have passed from death unto life, because we love the brethren." (1 John 3:14.)

A Regenerate man *has a special love for all true disciples of Christ.* Like his Father in heaven, he loves all men with a genuine **general** love—but he has a **special** love for those who are of one mind with himself. Like his Lord and Savior, he loves the worst of sinners, and could weep over them—but he has a peculiar love for those who are believers. He is never so much at home as when he is in their company. He is never so happy as when he is among the saints and the excellent of the earth. Others may value learning, or cleverness, or agreeableness, or riches, or rank—in the society they choose. The Regenerate man values grace. Those who have most grace, and are most like Christ, are those he loves most. He feels that they are members of the same family with himself, his brethren, his sisters, children of the same Father. He feels that they are fellow-soldiers fighting under the same captain, warring against the same enemy. He feels that they are his fellow-travelers, journeying along the same road, tried by the same difficulties, and soon about to rest with him in the same eternal home. He understands them, and they understand him. There is a kind of spiritual brotherhood between them. He and they may be very different in many ways—in rank, in station, in wealth. What does it matter? They are Jesus Christ's people. They are his Father's sons and daughters. Then he cannot help loving them.

Reader, I place this mark also before you. What would the Apostle say about you? Are you born of God?

5. Fifthly. John says, "Whoever is born of God overcomes the world." (1 John 5:4.)

A Regenerate man *does not make the world's opinion his rule of right and wrong.* He goes against the stream of the world's ways, notions, and customs. "What will men say?" is no longer a turning point with him. He overcomes the **love** of the world. He finds no pleasure in things which most around him call happiness. He cannot enjoy their enjoyments—they weary him; they appear to him vain, unprofitable, and unworthy of an immortal being. He overcomes the **fear** of the world. He is content to do many things which all around him think unnecessary, to say the least. They find fault with him—it does not move him. They ridicule him—he does not give way. He loves the praise of God more than the praise of man. He fears offending Him more than giving offence to man. He has counted the cost. He has taken his stand. It is a small thing with him now whether he is blamed or praised. His eye is upon Him who is invisible. He is resolved to follow Jesus wherever he goes. It may be necessary in this following to come out from the world and be separate. The Regenerate man will not shrink from doing so. Tell him that he is unlike other people, that his views are not the views of society generally, and that he is making himself singular and peculiar—you will not shake him. He is no longer the servant of fashion and custom. To please the world is quite a secondary consideration with him. His first aim is to please God.

Reader, I place this mark also before you. What would the Apostle say about you? Are you born of God?

6. Sixthly. John says, "He who was born of God keeps himself." (1 John 5:18.)

A Regenerate man is *very careful of his own soul*. He endeavors not only to keep clear of sin—but also to keep clear of everything which may lead to it. He is careful about the company he keeps. He feels that evil communications corrupt the heart, and that evil is far more catching than good, just as disease is more infectious than health. He is careful about the employment of his time—his chief desire about it is to spend it profitably. He is careful about the books he reads—he fears getting his mind poisoned by mischievous writings. He is careful about the friendships he forms—it is not enough for him that people are kind, and amiable, and good-natured—all this is very well—but will they do good to his soul? He is careful over his own daily habits and behavior—he tries to recollect that his own heart is deceitful, and that the world is full of wickedness, that the devil is always laboring to do him harm, and therefore he would sincerely be always on his guard. He desires to live like a soldier in an enemy's country, to wear his armor continually, and to be prepared for temptation. He finds by experience that his soul is ever among enemies, and he studies to be a watchful, humble, prayerful man.

Reader, I place this mark also before you. What would the Apostle say of you? Are you born of God?

Such are the six great marks of Regeneration, which God has given for our learning. Let everyone who has gone so far with me, read them over with attention, and lay them to heart. I believe they were written with the view to settle the great question of the present day, and intended to prevent disputes. Once more then, I ask the reader to mark and consider them.

I know there is a vast difference in the depth and distinctness of these marks among those who are Regenerate. In some people they are faint, dim, feeble, and hardly to be discerned. You almost need a microscope to make them out. In others they are bold, sharp, clear, plain, and un-mistakable, so that he who runs may read them. Some of these marks are more visible in some people, and others are more visible in others. It seldom happens that all are equally manifest in one and the same soul. All this I am quite ready to allow.

But still, after every allowance, here we find boldly painted the six marks of being born of God. Here are certain positive things laid down by John, as parts of the Regenerate man's character, as plainly and dis-tinctly as the features of a man's face. Here is an inspired Apostle writing one of the last general Epistles to the Church of Christ, telling us that a man born of God—

does not commit sin; believes that Jesus is the Christ; does righteous-ness; loves the brethren; overcomes the world; and keeps himself.

And more than once in the very same Epistle when these marks are mentioned, the Apostle tells us that he who has not this or that mark, is "not of God." I ask the reader to observe all this.

Now what shall we say to these things? What they can say who hold that Regeneration is only an admission to outward Church privileges, I am sure I do not know. For myself I say boldly, I can only come to one conclusion. That conclusion is, that those people only are regenerate who have these six marks about them, and that all men and women who have not these marks, are not regenerate, are not born again. And I firmly believe that this is the conclusion to which the Apostle wished us to come.

Reader, *have you these marks?* I know not what your opinions may be on this much-disputed subject of Regeneration. I know not on which side you may rank yourself. But once for all I warn you, if you find nothing in yourself answering to the marks I have been speaking of, you have reason indeed to be afraid. Without these marks it is vain to fancy you are Scripturally regenerate. The witness of the Apostle John is clear and express, that you are not. There must be a certain family likeness between God and His children. Without it you are none of His. There must be some visible evidence of the Spirit being within you, as plain as the stamp upon gold and silver, however small. Without this evidence you are only boasting of a false faith. Show me your faith without your works, said the Apostle James, when he wrote against those who are content with a dead faith. Show me your Regeneration without its fruits, is an argument that ought to be pressed home on many a conscience in the present day.

Reader, *if you have not these marks*, awake to a sense of your danger. Arise from your sleep of indifference and unconcern. Know the immense peril of hell and eternal misery in which you stand. Begin to use diligently every means by which God is ordinarily pleased to give grace to men's hearts, when they have not received it in their youth. Be diligent in hearing the Gospel preached. Be diligent in reading the Bible. Be diligent, above all, in prayer to the Lord Jesus Christ for the gift of the Holy Spirit.

If you take this course, I have every hope for you. None ever sought the Lord Jesus Christ in simplicity and sincerity—and sought in vain.

If, on the contrary, you refuse to take this course, and will continue as you are, I have little hope for you, and many fears. If the Bible be true, you are not yet born again. You will not use the most likely means to obtain this mighty blessing. What can I say but this, "the Lord have mercy upon your soul!"

Reader, *if you have these marks* I have been speaking of, be advised, and strive every year to make them more clear and plain. Let your repentance be a growing habit—your faith an increasing faith—your holiness a progressive holiness—your victory over the world a more decided victory—your love to the brethren a more hearty love—your watchfulness over yourself a more jealous watchfulness. Take this advice, and you will never repent of it. This is the way to be useful and happy in your religion. This is the way to put to silence the opposition of the enemies of truth. Let others, if they will, have Regeneration on their tongues, and nowhere else. Let it be your care to have it shining forth in your life, and to feel it in your heart.

Reader, I commend what I have been saying to your serious consideration. I believe that I have told you nothing but what is God's truth. You live in a day of gross darkness on the subject of Regeneration. Thousands are darkening God's counsel by confounding baptism and Regeneration. Beware of this. Keep the two subjects separate in your mind. Get clear views about Regeneration first of all, and then you are not likely to fall into mistakes about baptism. And when you have got clear views hold them fast—and never let them go!

Chapter Four

Alive or Dead?

"And He has made you alive, who were once dead in trespasses and sins." Ephesians 2:1

T he question which forms the title of this paper deserves a thousand thoughts. I invite every reader of this volume to look at it carefully, and ponder it well. Search your own heart, and do not lay down this book without solemn self-inquiry. Are you among the living, or among the dead?

Listen to me while I try to help you to an answer. Give me your attention, while I unfold this matter, and show you what God has said about it in the Scriptures. If I say hard things, it is not because I do not love you. I write as I do, because I desire your salvation. He is your best friend who tells you the most truth.

I. First then, let me tell you what we all are by nature. We are spiritually dead!

"Dead" is a strong word—but it is not my own coining and invention. I did not choose it. The Holy Spirit taught Paul to write it down about the Ephesians, ""And He has made you alive, who were once **dead** in trespasses and sins." The Lord Jesus Christ made use of it in the parable of the prodigal son, "This my son was *dead* and is alive again." (Luke 15:24, 32.) You will read it also in the first Epistle to Timothy, "She that lives in pleasure is *dead* while she lives." (1 Tim. 5:6.) Shall a mortal man be wise above that which is written? Must I not take heed to speak that which I find in the Bible, and neither less nor more?

"Dead" is an awful idea, and one that man is most unwilling to receive. He does not like to allow the whole extent of his soul's disease—he shuts his eyes to the real amount of his danger. Many a one will allow us to say, that naturally most people "are not quite what they ought to be—they are thoughtless—they are unsteady—they are mirthful—they are wild—they are not serious enough." But dead? Oh, no! We must not mention it. It is going too far to say that. The idea is a stone of stumbling, and a rock of offence."

"This is the reason we are no better, because our disease is not perfectly known—this is the reason we are no better, because we know not how bad we are."—*Usher's Sermons, preached at Oxford,* 1650.

But what we like in religion is of very little consequence. The only question is, What is written? What says the Lord? God's thoughts are not man's thoughts, and God's words are not man's words. God says of every living person who is not a real, thorough, genuine, decided Christian, be he high or low, rich or poor, old or young—*he is spiritually dead.*

In this, as in everything else, God's words are right. Nothing could be said more correct, nothing more accurate, nothing more faithful, nothing more true. Stay a little, and let me reason this out with you. Come and see.

What would you have said, if you had seen Joseph weeping over his father Jacob? "He fell upon his face, and wept upon him, and kissed him." (Gen. 50:1.) But there was no reply to his affection. All about that aged countenance was unmoved, silent, and still. Doubtless you would have guessed the reason. Jacob was dead.

What would you have said, if you had heard the Levite speaking to his wife, when he found her lying before the door in Gibeah? "Up," he said, "and let us be going. But she did not answer." (Judges 19:28.) His words were thrown away. There she lay, motionless, stiff, and cold. You know the cause. She was dead.

What would you have thought, if you had seen the Amalekite stripping Saul of his royal ornaments in Mount Gilboa? He "took from him the crown that was upon his head, and the bracelet that was on his arm." (2 Sam. 1:10.) There was no resistance. Not a muscle moved in that proud face—not a finger was raised to prevent him. And why? Saul was dead.

What would you have thought, if you had met the widow's son in the gate of Nain, lying in a coffin, wrapped about with grave-clothes, followed by his weeping mother, carried slowly towards the tomb? (Luke 7:12.) Doubtless it would have been all clear to you. It would have needed no explanation. The young man was dead.

Now I say this is just the condition of every man by nature in the matter of his soul. I say this is just the state of the vast majority of people around us in spiritual things. God calls to them continually—by mercies, by afflictions, by ministers, by His word—but they do not hear His voice. The Lord Jesus Christ mourns over them, pleads with them, sends them gracious invitations, knocks at the door of their hearts—but they do not regard it. The crown and glory of their being, that precious jewel, their immortal soul, is being seized, plundered, and taken away—and they are utterly unconcerned. The devil is carrying them away, day after day, along the broad road that leads to destruction—and they allow him to make them his captives without a struggle. And this is going on everywhere—all around us—among all classes—throughout the length and breadth of the land. You know it in your own conscience while you read this paper—you must be aware of it. You cannot deny it. And what then, I ask, can be said more perfectly true than that which God says—we are all by nature spiritually *dead?*

Yes! when a man's heart is cold and unconcerned about religion—when his hands are never employed in doing God's work—when his feet are not familiar with God's ways—when his tongue is seldom or never used in prayer and praise—when his ears are deaf to the voice of Christ in the Gospel—when his eyes are blind to the beauty of the kingdom of heaven—when his mind is full of the world, and has no room for spiritual things—when these marks are to be found in a man, the word of the Bible is the right word to use about him—and that word is, "Dead."

We may not like this perhaps. We may shut our eyes both to facts in the world, and texts in the Word. But God's truth must be spoken, and to keep it back does positive harm. Truth must be spoken, however condemning it may be. So long as a man does not serve God with body, soul, and spirit, he is not really alive. So long as he puts the first things last and the last first, buries his talent like an unprofitable servant, and brings the Lord no revenue of honor, so long in God's sight he is dead. He is not filling the place in creation for which he was intended; he is not using his powers and faculties as God meant them to be used. The poet's words are strictly true—

"He only lives, who lives to God, And all are dead beside."

This is the true explanation of sin not felt, and sermons not believed—and good advice not followed—and the Gospel not embraced—and the world not forsaken—and the cross not taken up—and self-will not mortified—and evil habits not laid aside—and the Bible seldom read—and the knee never bent in prayer. Why is all this on every side. The answer is simple—*Men are dead!*

This is the true account of that army of excuses, which so many make "with one consent." Some have no learning, and some have no time. Some are consumed with business and the care of money, and some with poverty. Some have difficulties in their own families, and some in their own health. Some have peculiar obstacles in their calling, which others, we are told, cannot understand; and others have peculiar drawbacks at home, and they wait to have them removed. But God has a shorter word in the Bible, which describes all these people at once. He says, *They are dead.* If spiritual life began in these people's hearts, their excuses would soon vanish away.

This is the true explanation of many things which wring a faithful minister's heart. Many around him never attend a place of worship at all. Many attend so irregularly, that it is clear they think it of no importance. Many attend once on a Sunday who might just as easily attend twice. Many never come to the Lord's table—and never appear at a weekday means of grace of any kind. And why is all this? Often, far too often, there can be only one reply about these people—*They are dead.*

See now how all professing Christians should examine themselves and try their own state. It is not in churchyards alone where the dead are to be found; there are only too many inside our churches, and close to our pulpits—too many on the benches, and too many in the pews. The land is like the valley in Ezekiel's vision, "full of bones, very many, and very dry." (Ezek. 37:2) There are dead souls in all our parishes, and dead souls in all our streets. There is hardly a family in which all live to God; there is hardly a house in which there is not someone dead. Oh, let us all search and look at home! Let us prove our own selves. Are we *alive or dead?*

See, too, how sad is the condition of all who have gone through no spiritual change, whose hearts are still the same as in the day they were born. There is a mountain of division between them and heaven. They have yet to "pass from death to life." (1 John 3:14.) Oh, that they did but see and know their danger! Alas, it is one fearful mark of spiritual death, that, like natural death—it is not felt! We lay our beloved ones tenderly and gently in their narrow beds—but they feel nothing of what we do. "The dead," says the wise man, "know nothing." (Eccl. 9:5.) And this is just the case with *dead souls.*

See, too, what reason ministers have to be anxious about their congregations. We feel that time is short, and life uncertain. We know that death spiritual is the high road that leads to death eternal. We fear lest any of our hearers should die in their sins, unprepared, unrenewed, impenitent, unchanged. Oh, marvel not if we often speak strongly and plead with you warmly! We dare not give you flattering titles, amuse you with trifles, say smooth things, and cry "Peace, peace," when life and death are at stake, and nothing less. The plague is among you. We feel that we stand between the living and the dead. We must and will "use great plainness of speech." "If the trumpet gives an uncertain sound, who shall prepare himself for the battle?" (2 Cor. 3:12; 1 Cor. 14:8.)

II. Let me tell you, in the second place, what every man needs who would be saved. *He must be quickened and made spiritually alive.*

Life is the mightiest of all possessions. From death to life is the mightiest of all changes. And no change short of this will ever avail to fit man's soul for heaven. Yes! it is not a little mending and alteration—a little cleansing and purifying—a little painting and patching—a little whitewashing and varnishing—a little turning over a new leaf and putting on a new outside that is needed. It is the bringing in of something altogether new—the planting within us of a new nature, a new being—a new principle—a new mind. This alone, and nothing less than this, will ever meet the necessities of man's soul. We need not merely a new skin—but a new heart.

"It is not a little reforming will save the man, no, nor all the morality in the world, nor all the common graces of God's spirit, nor the outward change of the life; they will not do, unless we are quickened, and have a new life wrought in us."—*Usher's Sermons.*

To hew a block of marble from the quarry—and carve it into a noble statue; to break up a waste wilderness—and turn it into a garden of flowers; to melt a lump of ironstone—and forgo it into watch-springs—all these are mighty changes. Yet they all come short of the change which every child of Adam requires, for they are merely the same thing in a new form, and the same substance in a new shape. But man requires the grafting in of that which he had not before. He needs a change as great as a resurrection from the dead—he must become a new creature. "Old things must pass away, and all things must become new." He must be "born again, born from above, born of God." The natural birth is not a whit more necessary to the life of the body, than is the spiritual birth to the life of the soul. (2 Cor. 5:17. John 3:3.)

I know well this is a hard saying. I know the children of this world dislike to hear that they must be born again. It pricks their consciences—it makes them feel they are further off from heaven than they are willing to allow. It seems like a narrow door which they have not yet stooped to enter, and they would gladly make the door wider, or climb in some other way. But I dare not give place by subjection in this matter. I will not foster a delusion, and tell people they only need repent a little, and stir up a gift they have within them, in order to become real Christians. I dare not use any other language than that of the Bible; and I say, in the words which are written for our learning, "We all need to be born again—we are all naturally dead, and must be made alive."

If we had seen Manasseh, King of Judah, at one time filling Jerusalem with idols, and murdering his children in honor of false gods—and then at another time purifying the temple, putting down idolatry, and living a godly life; if we had seen Zacchaeus the publican of Jericho, at one time cheating, plundering, and covetous—at another following Christ, and giving half his goods to the poor; if we had seen the servants of Nero's household, at one time conforming to their master's profligate ways—at another of one heart and mind with the Apostle Paul; if we had seen the ancient father Augustine, at one time living in fornication—at another walking closely with God; if we had seen our own Reformer Latimer, at one time preaching earnestly against the truth as it is in Jesus—at another spending and being spent even to death in Christ's cause; if we had seen the New Zealanders, or Tinnevelly Hindus, at one time blood-thirsty, immoral, or sunk in abominable superstitions—at another holy, pure, and believing Christians; if we had seen these wonderful changes, or any of them, I ask any sensible Christian what we would have said? Would we have been content to call them nothing more than amendments and alterations? would we have been satisfied with saying that Augustine had "reformed his ways," and that Latimer had "turned over a new leaf"? Verily if we said no more than this, the very stones would cry out. I say in all these cases there was nothing less than a new birth, a resurrection of human nature, a quickening of the dead. These are the right words to use. All other language is weak, poor, beggarly, unscriptural, and short of the truth.

Now I will not shrink from saying plainly, we all need the same kind of change, if we are to be saved. The difference between us and any of those I have just named is far less than it appears. Take off the outward crust, and you will find the same nature beneath, in us and them—an evil nature, requiring a complete change. The face of the earth is very different in different climates—but the heart of the earth, I believe, is everywhere the same. Go where you will, from one end to the other, you would always find the granite, or other primitive rocks, beneath your feet, if you only bored down deep enough. And it is just the same with men's hearts. Their customs and their colors, their ways and their laws, may all be utterly unlike; but the inner man is always the same. Their hearts are all alike at the bottom—all stony, all hard, all ungodly, all needing to be thoroughly renewed. The Englishman and the New Zealander stand on the same level in this matter. Both are naturally dead, and both need to be made alive. Both are children of the same father Adam who fell by sin, and both need to be "born again," and made children of God.

Whatever part of the globe we live in, our eyes need to be opened—naturally we never see our sinfulness, guilt, and danger. Whatever nation we belong to our understandings need to be enlightened—naturally we know little or nothing of the plan of salvation—like the Babel-builders, we think to get to heaven our own way. Whatever church we may belong to, our wills need to be bent in the right direction—naturally we would never choose the things which are for our peace; we would never come to Christ. Whatever be our rank in life, our affections need to be turned to things above—naturally we only set them on things below, earthly, sensual, short-lived, and vain. Pride must give place to humility—self-righteousness to self-abasement—carelessness to seriousness—worldliness to holiness—unbelief to faith. Satan's dominion must be put down within us, and the kingdom of God set up. Self must be crucified, and Christ must reign. Until these things come to pass, we are dead as stones. When these things begin to take place, and not until then, we are spiritually alive.

> "Man's understanding is so darkened that he can see nothing of God in God, nothing of holiness in holiness, nothing of good in good, nothing of evil in evil, nor anything of sinfulness in sin. Nay, it is so darkened that he fancies himself to see good in evil, and evil in good, happiness in sin, and misery in holiness." —*Berridge*

I dare say this sounds like foolishness to some. But many a living man could stand up this day and testify that it is true. Many an one could tell us that he knows it all by experience, and that he does indeed feel himself a new man. He loves the things that once he hated, and hates the things that once he loved. He has new habits, new companions, new ways, new tastes, new feelings, new opinions, new sorrows, new joys, new anxieties, new pleasures, new hopes, and new fears. In short, the whole bias and current of his being is changed. Ask his nearest relations and friends, and they would bear witness to it. Whether they liked it or not, they would be obliged to confess he was no longer the same.

> "How wonderfully does the new born soul differ from his former self. He lives a new life, he walks in a new way, he steers his course by a new compass, and towards a new coast. His principle is new, his pattern is new, his practices are new, his projects are new, all is new. He ravels out all he had wove before, and employs himself wholly about another work." —*George Swinnocke.* 1660.

Many a one could tell you that once he did not think himself such a very great transgressor. At any rate he fancied he was no worse than others. Now he would say with the apostle Paul, he feels himself the "chief of sinners." (1 Tim. 1. 15.)

> "I cannot pray—but I sin—I cannot hear or preach a sermon—but I sin—I cannot give an alms, or receive the sacrament—but I sin—nay, I cannot so much as confess my sins—but my confessions are still aggravations of them. My repentance needs to be repented of, my tears want washing, and the very washing of my tears needs still to be washed over again with the blood of my Redeemer."—*Beveridge.*

> "Woe is me, that man should think there is anything in me! He is my witness, before whom I am as crystal, that the secret house-devils, that bear me too often company, that the corruption which I find within, make me go with low sails."—*Rutherford's Letters.* 1637.

Once he did not consider he had a bad heart. He might have his faults, and be led away by bad company and temptations—but 'he had a good heart at the bottom'. Now he would tell you, he knows no heart so bad as his own. He finds it "deceitful above all things, and desperately wicked." (Jer. 17:6.)

Once he did not suppose it was a very hard matter to get to heaven. He thought he had only to repent, and say a few prayers, and do what he could, and Christ would make up what was lacking. Now he believes the way is narrow, and few find it. He is convinced he could never have made his own peace with God. He is persuaded that nothing but the blood of Christ could wash away his sins. His only hope is to be "justified by faith without the deeds of the law." (Rom. 3:28.)

Once he could see no beauty and excellence in the Lord Jesus Christ. He could not understand some ministers speaking so much about Him. Now he would tell you He is the pearl above all price, the chief among ten thousand, his Redeemer, his Advocate, his Priest, his King, his Physician, his Shepherd, his Friend, his All.

Once he thought lightly about sin. He could not see the necessity of being so particular about it. He could not think a man's words, and thoughts, and actions, were of such importance, and required such watchfulness. Now he would tell you sin is the abominable thing which he hates, the sorrow and burden of his life. He longs to be more holy. He can enter thoroughly into Whitefield's desire, "I want to go where I shall neither sin myself, nor see others sin any more."

> "I am sick of all I do, and stand astonished that the Redeemer still continues to make use of and bless me. Surely I am more foolish than any man—no one receives so much and does so little."—Whitefield's Letters.

Once he found no pleasure in means of grace. The Bible was neglected. His prayers, if he had any, were a mere form. Sunday was a tiresome day. Sermons were a weariness, and often sent him to sleep. Now all is altered. These things are the food, the comfort, the delight of his soul.

Once he disliked earnest-minded Christians. He shunned them as melancholy, low-spirited, weak people. Now they are the excellent of the earth, of whom he cannot see too much. He is never so happy as he is in their company. He feels if all men and women were saints, it would be heaven upon earth.

Once he cared only for this world, its pleasures, its business, its occupations, its rewards. Now he looks upon it as an empty, unsatisfying place; an inn—a lodging—a training-school for the life to come. His treasure is in heaven. His home is beyond the grave.

I ask once more, what is all this but new life? Such a change as I have described is no vision and fancy. It is a real actual thing, which not a few in this world have known or felt. It is not a picture of my own imagining. It is a true thing which some of us could find at this moment hard by our own doors. But wherever such a change does take place, there you see the thing of which I am now speaking—you see the *dead made alive,* a new creature, a soul born again. "So that if any one is in Christ, that one is a new creature; old things have passed away; behold, all things have become new." (2 Corinthians 5:17)

I would to God that changes such as this were more common! I would to God there were not such multitudes, of whom we must say even weeping, they know nothing about the matter at all. But, common or not, one thing I say plainly, this is the kind of change we all need. I do not hold that all must have exactly the same experience. I allow most fully that the change is different, in degree, extent, and intensity, in different people. Grace may be weak, and yet true—life may be feeble, and yet real. But I do confidently affirm we must all go through something of this kind, if ever we mean to be saved. Until this sort of change has taken place, there is no life in us at all. We may be living Churchmen—but we are dead Christians.

> "If we be still our old selves, no changelings at all, the same
> man that we came into the world, without mortification

of our corruptions, without addition of grace and sanctification, surely we must seek us another Father, we are not
yet the sons of God."—Hall, 1652.

"If you have anything less than regeneration, believe me,
you can never see heaven. There is no hope of heaven until
then—until you are born again."—*Usher's Sermons.*

Take it home, every man or woman that reads this paper, take it home
to your own conscience, and look at it well. Some time or other, between
the cradle and the grave, all who would be saved must be made alive.
The words which good old Berridge had engraved on his tombstone are
faithful and true, "Reader! are you born again? Remember! no salvation
without a new birth."

See now what an amazing gulf there is between the Christian in name
and form—and the Christian in deed and truth. It is not the difference of
one being a little better, and the other a little worse than his neighbor—it
is the difference between a state of life and a state of death. The smallest
blade of grass that grows upon a Highland mountain is a more noble
object than the fairest wax flower that was ever formed; for it has that
which no science of man can impart—has *life.* The most splendid marble
statue in Greece or Italy is nothing by the side of the poor sickly child that
crawls over the cottage floor; for with all its beauty it is *dead.* And the
weakest member of the family of Christ is far higher and more precious
in God's eyes than the most gifted man of the world. The one lives unto
God, and shall live forever—the other, with all his intellect, is still dead
in sins.

Oh, you that have passed from death to life, you have reason indeed
to be thankful! Remember what you once were by nature—dead. Think

what you are now by grace—alive. Look at the dry bones thrown up from the graves. Such were you; and who has made you to differ? Go and fall low before the footstool of your God. Bless Him for His grace, His free distinguishing grace. Say to Him often, "Who am I, Lord, that you have brought me hitherto? Why me? Why have you been merciful unto me?"

III. Let me tell you, in the third place—in what way alone this quickening can be brought about—by what means a dead soul can be made spiritually alive.

Surely, if I did not tell you this, it would be cruelty to write what I have written. Surely, it would be leading you into a dreary wilderness, and then leaving you without bread and water. It would be like marching you down to the Red Sea, and then bidding you walk over. It would be commanding you to make brick like Pharaoh, and yet refusing to provide you with straw. It would be like tying your hands and feet, and then desiring you to fight a good warfare, and "so run as to obtain the prize." I will not do so. I will not leave you, until I have pointed out the wicket-gate towards which you must run. By God's help, I will set before you the full provision there is made for dead souls. Listen to me a little longer, and I will once more show you what is written in the Scripture of truth.

One thing is very clear—**we cannot work this mighty change ourselves.** It is not in us. We have no strength or power to do it. We may change our sins—but we cannot change our hearts. We may take up a new way—but not a new nature. We may make considerable reforms and alterations. We may lay aside many outward bad habits, and begin to do many outward duties. But we cannot create a new principle within us. We cannot bring something out of nothing. The Ethiopian cannot change his skin, nor the leopard his spots. No more can we put life into our own souls. (Jerem. 13:23.)

"There is not one good duty which the natural man can do. If it should be said to him, Think but one good thought, and for it you shall go to heaven, he could not think it. Until God raises him from the sink of sin, as He did Lazarus from the grave, he cannot do anything that is well pleasing to God. He may do the works of a moral man—but to do the works of a man quickened and enlightened, is beyond his power."—*Usher's Sermons.*

> "Nature can no more cast out nature, than Satan can cast out Satan."—*Thomas Watson,* 1653.

> "Nature cannot raise itself to this, any more than a man can give natural being to himself."—*Leighton.*

Another thing is equally clear; no other man can do it for us. Ministers may preach to us, and pray with us—receive us at the font in baptism, admit us at the Lord's Table, and give us the bread and wine—but they cannot bestow spiritual life. They may bring in regularity in the place of disorder, and outward decency in the place of open sin. But they cannot go below the surface. They cannot reach our hearts. Paul may plant and Apollos water—but God alone can give the increase. (1 Cor. 3:6.) Who then can make a dead soul alive? No one can do it but God. He only who breathed into Adam's nostrils the breath of life, can ever make a dead sinner—a living Christian. He only who formed the world out of nothing in the day of creation, can make man a new creature. He only who said, "Let there be light, and there was light," can cause spiritual light to shine into man's heart. He only who formed man out of the dust and gave life to his body can ever give life to his soul. His is the special office to do it by His Spirit, and His also is the power. (Gen. 1:2, 3.)

"To create or bring something out of nothing, is beyond the power of the strongest creature. It is above the
strength of all people and angels to create the least blade of
grass; God challenges this as His prerogative royal. (Isaiah
40:26.) Augustine said truly, To convert the little world
'man' is more than to create the great world."—*George
Swinnocke,* 1660.

The glorious Gospel contains provision for our spiritual, as well as
our eternal life. The Lord Jesus is a complete Savior. That mighty living
Head has no dead members. His people are not only justified and pardoned—but quickened together with Him, and made partakers of His
resurrection. To Him the Spirit joins the sinner, and raises him by that
union from death to life. In Him the sinner lives after he has believed.
The spring of all his vitality is the union between Christ and his soul,
which the Spirit begins and keeps up. Christ is the appointed fountain
of all spiritual life, and the Holy Spirit the appointed agent who conveys
that life to our souls.

"Then do we begin to live, when we begin to have union
with Christ the Fountain of Life, by His Spirit com-
municated to us—from this time we are to reckon our
life."—*Flavel.*

"Christ is an universal principle of all life."—*Sibbes.* 1635.

Come to the Lord Jesus Christ, if you would have life. He will not cast
you out. He has gifts, even for the rebellious. The moment the dead man

touched the body of Elisha, he revived and stood upon his feet. (2 Kings 13:21.)—The moment you touch the Lord Jesus with the hand of faith, you are alive unto God, as well as forgiven all trespasses. Come, and your soul shall live.

I never despair of anyone becoming a decided Christian, whatever he may have been in days gone by. I know how great the change is from death to life. I know the mountains of division that seem to stand between some of us and heaven. I know the hardness, the prejudices, the desperate sinfulness of the natural heart. But I remember that God the Father made this beautiful and well-ordered world out of nothing. I remember the voice of the Lord Jesus could reach Lazarus when four days dead, and recall him even from the grave. I remember the amazing victories the Spirit of God has won in every nation under heaven. I remember all this, and feel that I never need despair. Yes! those among us who now seem most utterly dead in sins, may yet be raised to a new being, and walk before God in newness of life.

Why should it not be so? The Holy Spirit is a merciful and loving Spirit. He turns away from no man because of his vileness. He passes by no one because his sins are black and scarlet. There was nothing in the Corinthians that He should come down and quicken them. Paul reports of them that they were "fornicators, idolaters, adulterers, homosexuals, thieves, covetous, drunkards, revilers, extortioners." "Such," he says, "were some of you." Yet even them the Spirit made alive. "You are washed," he writes, "you are sanctified, you are justified, in the name of the Lord Jesus, and by the Spirit of our God." (1 Cor. 6:9-11.)

There was nothing in the Colossians, that He should visit their hearts. Paul tells us that "they walked in sexual immorality, impurity, lust, evil desire, and covetousness, which is idolatry." Yet them also the Spirit quickened. He made them "put off the old man with his deeds, and put on the new man which is renewed in knowledge after the image of Him that created him." (Coloss. 3:5-10.)

There was nothing in Mary Magdalene that the Spirit should make her soul alive. Once she had been "possessed with seven devils." There was once a time, if report be true, when she was a woman proverbial for vileness and iniquity. Yet even her the Spirit made a new creature, separated her from her sins, brought her to Christ, made her "last at the cross, and first at the tomb."

Never, never will the Spirit turn away from a soul because of its corruption. He never has done so—He never will. It is His glory that He has purified the minds of the most impure, and made them temples for His own abode. He may yet take the worst of us, and make him a vessel of grace.

Why indeed should it not be so? The Spirit is an Almighty Spirit. He can change the stony heart into a heart of flesh. He can break up and destroy the strongest bad habits, like string in the fire. He can make the most difficult things seem easy, and the mightiest objections melt away like snow in spring. He can cut the bars of brass, and throw the gates of prejudice wide open. He can fill up every valley, and make every rough place smooth. He has done it often, and He can do it again.

"Such is the power of the Holy Spirit to regenerate people, and as it were to bring them forth anew, so that they shall be nothing like the people they were before."

The Spirit can take a Jew—the bitterest enemy of Christianity, the fiercest persecutor of true believers—the strongest stickler for Pharisaical notions, the most prejudiced opposer of Gospel doctrine—and turn that man into an earnest preacher of the very faith he once destroyed. He has done it already. He did it with the Apostle Paul.

The Spirit can take a Roman Catholic monk, brought up in the midst of Romish superstition—trained from his infancy to believe false doctrine, and obey the Pope—steeped to the eyes in error, and make that man the clearest upholder of justification by faith the world ever saw. He has done so already. He did it with Martin Luther.

The Spirit can take an English tinker, without learning, patronage, or money—a man at one time notorious for nothing so much as blasphemy and swearing—and make that man write a pious book, which shall stand unrivaled and unequaled, in its way, by any book since the time of the Apostles. He has done so already. He did it with John Bunyan, the author of "Pilgrim's Progress."

The Spirit can take a sailor drenched in worldliness and sin—a profligate captain of a slave ship, and make that man a most successful minister of the Gospel—a writer of godly letters, which are a storehouse of experimental religion—and of hymns which are known and sung wherever English is spoken. He has done it already. He did it with John Newton.

All this the Spirit has done, and much more, of which I cannot speak particularly. And the arm of the Spirit is not shortened. His power is not decayed. He is like the Lord Jesus, the same yesterday, today, and forever." (Heb. 13:8.) He is still doing wonders, and will do to the very end.

Once more then, I say, I never despair of any man's soul being made alive. I would despair—if it depended on man himself. Some seem so hardened, I would have no hope. I would despair if it depended on the work of ministers. Alas, the very best of us are poor, weak creatures! But I cannot despair when I remember that God the Spirit is the agent who conveys life to the soul—for I know and am persuaded that with Him nothing is impossible.

I would not be surprised to hear, even in this life, that the hardest man in the list of my acquaintances has become softened, and the proudest has taken his place at the feet of Jesus as a weaned child.

I shall not be surprised to meet many on the right hand, in the day of judgment, whom I shall leave, when I die, traveling in the broad way to destruction. I shall be startled, and say, "What! you here!" I shall only remind them, "Was not this my word, when I was yet among you—Nothing is impossible with Him who quickens the dead."

Does anyone of us desire to help the Church of Christ? Then let him pray for a great outpouring of the Spirit. Only the Holy Spirit can give edge to sermons, and point to advice, and power to rebukes, and can cast down the high walls of sinful hearts. It is not better preaching, and finer writing that is needed in this day—but more of the presence of the Holy Spirit.

Does anyone feel the slightest drawing towards God—the smallest concern about his immortal soul? Then flee to that open fountain of living waters, the Lord Jesus Christ, and you shall receive the Holy Spirit. (John 7:39.) Begin at once to pray for the Holy Spirit. Think not that you are shut up and cut off from hope. The Holy Spirit is promised to "those who ask Him." (Luke 11:13.) His very name is the Spirit of promise and the Spirit of life. Give Him no rest until He comes down and makes you a new heart. Cry mightily unto the Lord—say unto Him, "Bless me, even me also—quicken me, and make me alive."

And now let me wind up all I have said with a few words of **special application**. I have shown what I believe to be the truth as it is in Jesus. Let me try, by God's blessing, to bring it home to the hearts and consciences of all into whose hands this volume may fall.

1. First, let me put this question to every soul who reads this paper, "Are you dead, or are you alive?"

Allow me, as an ambassador for Christ, to press the inquiry on every conscience. There are only two **ways** to walk in, the narrow way and the broad way. There are only two **companies** in the day of judgment, those on the right hand, and those on the left. There are only two **classes** of people in the professing Church of Christ, and to one of them you must belong. Where are you? What are you? Are you among the living, or among the dead?

I speak to you yourself, and to none else—not to your neighbor—but to you, not to Africans or New Zealanders—but to you. I do not ask whether you are an angel, or whether you have the mind of David or Paul—but I do ask whether you have a well-founded hope that you are a new creature in Christ Jesus, I do ask whether you have reason to believe you have put off the old man and put on the new—whether you are conscious of ever having gone through a real spiritual change of heart—whether, in one word, you are dead or alive.

"All hangs upon this hinge. If this be not done, you are undone—undone eternally. All your profession, civility, privileges, gifts, duties, are ciphers, and signify nothing, unless regeneration be the figure put before them. "—*Swinnocke*. 1660.

"Believe me, whatever you are, you shall never be saved for being a Lord or a knight, a gentleman or a rich man, a learned man or a well-spoken, eloquent man; nor yet for being a Calvinist, or a Lutheran, an Arminian, an Anabaptist, a Presbyterian, an Independent, or a Protestant, formally and merely as such; much less for being a Papist, or of any such grossly deluded sect—but as a regenerate

Christian it is that you must be saved—or you can have
no hope."—*Richard Baxter*. 1659.

(a) Think not to put me off by saying, "you were admitted into the
Church by baptism, you received grace and the Spirit in that sacrament,
you are alive." It shall not avail you. Paul himself says of the baptized
widow who lives in pleasure, "She is *dead* while she lives." (1 Tim. 5:6.)
The Lord Jesus Christ Himself tells the chief officer of the Church in
Sardis, "You have a name that you live, and are *dead.*" (Rev. 3:1.). The
life you talk of is nothing if it cannot be seen. Show it to me, if I am
to believe its existence. Grace is light, and light will always be discerned.
Grace is salt, and salt will always be tasted. An indwelling of the Spirit
which does not show itself by outward fruits, and a grace which men's
eyes cannot discover, are both to be viewed with the utmost suspicion.
Believe me, if you have no other proof of spiritual life but your baptism,
you are yet a dead soul.

(b) Think not to tell me "It is a question that cannot be decided,
and you call it presumptuous to give an opinion in such a matter." This
is a vain refuge, and a false humility. Spiritual life is no such dim and
doubtful thing as you seem to fancy. There are marks and evidences by
which its presence may be discerned by those who know the Bible. "We
know," says John, "that we have passed from death unto life." (1 John
3:14.) The exact time and season of that passage may often be hidden
from a man. The fact and reality of it will seldom be entirely an uncertain
thing. It was a true and beautiful saying of a Scotch girl, to Whitefield,
when asked if her heart was changed, "Something was changed, she knew,
it might be the world, it might be her own heart—but there was a great
change somewhere, she was quite sure, for everything seemed different

to what it once did." Oh, cease to evade the inquiry! "Anoint your eyes with eye-salve that you may see." (Rev. 3:18.) Are you dead or alive?

(c) Think not to reply, "You do not know—you allow it is a matter of importance—you hope to know some time before you die—you mean to give your mind to it when you have a convenient season—but at present you do not know." You do not know! Yet heaven or hell is wrapped up in this question. An eternity of happiness or misery hinges upon your answer. You do not leave your worldly affairs so unsettled. You do not manage your earthly business so loosely. You look far forward. You provide against every possible contingency. You insure life and property. Oh, why not deal in the same way with your immortal soul?

You do not know! Yet all around you is uncertainty. You are a poor frail worm—your body fearfully and wonderfully made—your health liable to be put out of order in a thousand ways. **The next time the daisies bloom, it may be over your grave!** All before you is dark. You know not what a day might bring forth, much less a year. Oh! why not bring your soul's business to a point without delay?

Let every reader of this paper begin the great business of self-examination. Rest not until you know the length and breadth of your own state in God's sight. Backwardness in this matter is an evil sign. It springs from an uneasy conscience. It shows that a man thinks ill of his own case. He feels, like a dishonest tradesman, that his accounts will not bear inquiry. He dreads the light.

In spiritual things, as in everything else, it is the highest wisdom to make sure work. Take nothing for granted. Do not measure your condition by that of others. Bring everything to the measure of God's Word. **A mistake about your soul is a mistake for eternity!** "Surely," says Leighton, "they that are not born again, shall one day wish they had never been born."

Sit down this day and think. Commune with your own heart and be still. Go to your own room and consider. Enter into your own closet, or at any rate contrive to be alone with God. Look the question fairly, fully, honestly in the face. How does it touch you? Are you among the living or among the dead?

> "If your state be good, searching into it will give you the comfort of it. If your state be bad, searching into it cannot make it worse; nay, it is the only way to make it better—for conversion begins with conviction."—*Hopkins.* 1680.

2. In the second place, let me speak in all affection to those who are DEAD.

What shall I say to you? What can I say? What words of mine are likely to have any effect on your hearts? This I will say—I mourn over your souls. I do most sincerely mourn. You may be thoughtless and unconcerned. You may care little for what I am saying. You may scarcely run your eye over this paper, and after reading it you may despise it and return to the world; but you cannot prevent my feeling for you, however little you may feel for yourselves.

Do I mourn when I see a young man sapping the foundation of his bodily health by indulging his lusts and passions, sowing bitterness for himself in his old age? Much more then will I mourn over your souls.

Do I mourn when I see people squandering away their inheritance, and wasting their property on trifles and follies? Much more then will I mourn over your souls.

Do I mourn when I hear of one drinking slow poisons, because they are pleasant, as the drunkard or the opium-eater—inch by inch digging his own grave? Much more then will I mourn over your souls.

I mourn to think of golden opportunities thrown away—of Christ rejected, of the blood of atonement trampled under foot—of the Spirit resisted; the Bible neglected—heaven despised, and the world put in the place of God.

I mourn to think of the present happiness you are missing, the peace and consolation you are thrusting from you, the misery you are laying up in store for yourselves—and the bitter waking up which is yet to come!

Yes! I must mourn. I cannot help it. Others may think it enough to mourn over dead bodies. For my part, I think there is far more cause to mourn over dead souls. The children of this world find fault with us sometimes for being so serious and grave. Truly, when I look at the world, I marvel we can ever smile at all.

To everyone who is dead in sins I say this day—Why will you die? Are the wages of sin so sweet and good, that you cannot give them up? Is the world so satisfying that you cannot forsake it? Is the service of Satan so pleasant that you and he are never to be parted? Is heaven so poor a thing that it is not worth seeking? Is your soul of so little consequence, that it is not worth a struggle to have it saved? Oh, turn! turn before it be too late! God is not willing that you should perish. "As I live," He says, "I have no pleasure in the death of him who dies." Jesus loves you, and grieves to see your folly. He wept over wicked Jerusalem, saying, "I would have gathered you—but you would not be gathered." Surely if lost, your blood will be upon your own heads. "Awake, and arise from the dead, and Christ shall give you light." (Ezek. 18"32; Matt. 23:37; Eph. 5:14.)

Believe me, believe me, true repentance is that one step that no man ever repented of. Thousands have said at their latter end, they had "served God too little." But no person ever said, as he left this world, that he had cared for his soul too much. The way of life is a narrow path—but the footsteps in it are all in one direction—not one child of Adam has ever come back and said it was a delusion. The way of the world is a broad way—but millions on millions have forsaken it, and borne their testimony that it was a way of sorrow and disappointment.

3. Let me, in the third place, speak to those who are living.

Are you indeed alive unto God? Can you say with truth, "I was dead, and am alive again. I was blind—but now I see"? Then allow the word of exhortation, and incline your hearts unto wisdom.

Are you alive? Then see that you *prove* it *by your actions.* Be a consistent witness. Let your words, and works, and ways, and tempers all tell the same story. Let not your life be a poor torpid life, like that of a tortoise or a sloth—let it rather be an energetic stirring life, like that of a deer or bird. Let your graces shine forth from all the windows of your life, that those who live near you may see that the Spirit is abiding in your hearts. Let your light not be a dim, flickering, uncertain flame; let it burn steadily, like the eternal fire on the altar, and never become low. Let the savor of your religion, like Mary's precious ointment, fill all the houses where you dwell. Be an epistle of Christ so clearly written, penned in such large bold characters—that he who runs may read it. Let your Christianity be so unmistakable, your eye so single, your heart so whole, your walk so straightforward that all who see you may have no doubt whose you are, and whom you serve. If we are quickened by the Spirit, no one ought to be able to doubt it. Our conversation should declare plainly that we "seek a country." (Heb 11:14.) It ought not to be necessary to tell people, as in the case of a badly painted picture, "This is a Christian." We ought not to be so sluggish and still, that people shall be obliged to come close and look hard, and say, "Is he dead or alive?"

Are you alive? Then see that you *prove* it *by your growth.* Let the great change within become every year more evident. Let your light be an increasing light, not like Joshua's sun in the valley of Ajalon, standing still—nor like Hezekiah's sun, going backwards—but ever shining more and more to the very end of your days. Let the image of your Lord, wherein you are renewed, grow clearer and sharper every month. Let it not be like the image and superscription on a coin, more indistinct and defaced the longer it is used. Let it rather become more plain the older it is, and let the likeness of your King stand out more fully and sharply.

I have no confidence in a standing-still religion. I do not think a Christian was meant to be like an animal, to grow to a certain age, and then stop growing. I believe rather he was meant to be like a tree, and to increase more and more in strength and vigor all his days. Remember the words of the Apostle Peter, *"Add* to your faith virtue, and to virtue knowledge, and to knowledge temperance, and to temperance brotherly kindness, and to brotherly kindness charity." (2 Peter 1:5, 6, 7.) This is the way to be a useful Christian. People will believe you are in earnest when they see constant improvement, and perhaps be drawn to go with you. This is one way to obtain comfortable assurance. "So an entrance shall be ministered unto you abundantly." (2 Peter 1:11.) Oh, as ever you would be useful and happy in your religion, let your motto be, "Forward, forward!" to your very last day.

> "People observe *actions,* a great deal more than *words.*"
> —*Leighton.*

I entreat all believing readers to remember that I speak to myself as well as to them. I say the spiritual life there is in Christians ought to be more evident. Our lamps need trimming—they ought not to burn so dim. Our separation from the world should be more distinct—our walk with God more decided. Too many of us are like Lot—lingerers; or like Reuben, Gad, and Manasseh—borderers; or like the Jews in Ezra's time—so mixed up with strangers, that our spiritual pedigree cannot be made out. It ought not so to be. Let us be up and doing. If we live in the Spirit, let us also walk in the Spirit. If we really have life, let us make it known.

The state of the world demands it. The latter days have fallen upon us. The kingdoms of the earth are shaking, falling, crashing, and crumbling away. (Isaiah 24:1, etc.) The glorious kingdom that will never be removed is drawing near. The King Himself is close at hand. The children of this world are looking round to see what the saints are doing. God, in His wonderful providences, is calling to us, "Who is on my side? Who?"—Surely we ought to be, like Abraham, very ready with our answer, "Here am I!" (Gen. 22:1.)

"Ah!" you may say, "These are ancient things—these are brave words. We know it all. But we are weak, we have no power to think a good thought, we can do nothing, we must sit still." Hearken, my believing reader. What is the cause of your weakness? Is it not because the fountain of life is little used? Is it not because you are resting on old experiences, and not daily gathering new manna—daily drawing new strength from Christ? He has left you the promise of the Comforter. "He gives more grace"—grace upon grace to all who ask it. He came "that you might have life, and have it more abundantly." "Open your mouths wide," He says this day, "and they shall be filled." (James 4:6; John 10:10; Ps. 81:10.)

I say to all believers who read this paper, if you want your spiritual life to be more healthy and vigorous, you must just come more boldly to the throne of grace. You must give up this hanging-back spirit—this hesitation about taking the Lord at His own word. Doubtless you are poor sinners, and nothing at all. The Lord knows it, and has provided a store of strength for you. But you do not draw upon the store He has provided—you have not, because you ask not. The secret of your weakness is your little faith—and little prayer. The fountain is unsealed—but you only sip a few drops. The bread of life is before you—yet you only eat a few crumbs. The treasury of heaven is open—but you only take a few pennies. "O you of little faith, why do you doubt?" (Matt. 14:31.)

Awake to know your privileges—awake, and sleep no longer. Tell me not of spiritual hunger, and thirst, and poverty—so long as the throne of grace is before you. Say rather, that you are proud—and will not come to it as poor sinners. Say rather, you are slothful—and will not take pains to get more.

Cast aside the grave-clothes of pride—which still hang around you. Throw off that Egyptian garment of indolence—which ought not to have been brought through the Red Sea. Away with that unbelief, which ties and paralyzes your tongue. You are not straitened in God—but in yourselves. "Come boldly to the throne of grace," where the Father is ever waiting to give, and Jesus ever sits by Him to intercede. (Heb. 4:16.) Come boldly, for you may, all sinful as you are—if you come in the name of the Great High Priest. Come boldly, and ask largely, and you shall have abundant answers—mercy like a river, and grace and strength like a mighty stream. Come boldly, and you shall have supplies exceeding all you can ask or think. "Hitherto you have asked nothing. Ask and receive, that your joy may be full." (John 16:24.)

If we really are *alive and not dead,* let us strive so to carry ourselves that people may know whose we are. While we live, may we live unto the Lord. When we die, may we die the death of the righteous. And when the Lord Jesus comes, may we be found ready, and "not be ashamed before Him at His coming." (1 John 2:28.)

But, after all, are we alive or dead? That is the great question!

Chapter Five

Having the Spirit

"Worldly people, who do not have the Spirit." - Jude 19

I take it for granted that every reader of this paper believes in the Holy Spirit. The number of people in this country who are infidels, deists, or Socinians, and openly deny the doctrine of the Trinity, is happily not very great. Most people have been baptized in the name of the Father, and of the Son, and of the Holy Spirit. There are few Churchmen, at any rate, who have not often heard the well-known words of our old Catechism, "I believe in God the Holy Spirit, who sanctifies me and all the elect people of God."

But, notwithstanding all this, it would be well for many if they would consider what they know of the Holy Spirit beyond His name. What experimental acquaintance have you with the Spirit's work? What has He done for you? What benefit have you received from Him? You can say of God the Father, "He made me and all the world." You can say of God the Son, "He died for me and all mankind." But can you say anything about the Holy Spirit? Can you say, with any degree of confidence, "He dwells in me, and sanctifies me"? In one word, Have you the Spirit? The text which heads this paper will tell you that there is such a thing as "not having the Spirit." This is the point which I press upon your attention.

I believe the point to be one of vital importance at all seasons. I hold it to be one of special importance in the present day. I consider that clear views about the work of the Holy Spirit are among the best preservatives against the many false doctrines which abound in our times. Allow me then, to lay before you a few things, which by God's blessing, may throw light on the subject of having the Spirit.

I. Let me explain the immense importance of "Having the Spirit."

II. Let me point out the great general principle by which alone the question can be tried, "Have you the Spirit?"

III. Let me describe the particular effects which the Spirit always produces on the souls in which He dwells.

I. Let me, in the first place, explain the immense importance of having the Spirit.

It is absolutely necessary to make this point clear. Unless you see this, I shall appear like one beating the air all through this paper. Once let your mind lay hold on this, and half the work I want to do is already done for your soul.

I can easily fancy some reader saying, I do not see the use of this question! Supposing I have not the Spirit, what is the mighty harm? I try to do my duty in this world—I attend my church regularly—I receive the Sacrament occasionally—I believe I am as good a Christian as my neighbors. I say my prayers—I trust God will pardon my sins for Christ's sake. I do not see why I should not reach heaven at last, without troubling myself with hard questions about the Spirit."

If these are your thoughts, I entreat you to give me your attention for a few minutes, while I try to supply you with reasons for thinking differently. Believe me, nothing less than your soul's salvation depends on "Having the Spirit." Life or death; heaven or hell; eternal happiness or eternal misery; are bound up with the subject of this paper.

(a) Remember, for one thing, **if you have not the Spirit, you have no part in Christ, and no title to heaven.**

The words of Paul are express and unmistakable, "If any man has not the Spirit of Christ, he does not belong to Him." (Rom. 8:9.) The words of John are no less clear, "Hereby we know that He abides in us by the Spirit whom He has given us." (1 John 3:24.) The indwelling of God the Holy Spirit is the common mark of all true believers in Christ. It is the Shepherd's mark on the flock of the Lord Jesus, distinguishing them from the rest of the world. It is the goldsmith's stamp on the genuine sons of God, which separates them from the dross and mass of false professors. It is the King's own seal on those who are His peculiar people, proving them to be His own property. It is "the pledge" which the Redeemer gives to His believing disciples while they are in the body, as a token of the full and complete "redemption" yet to come in the resurrection morning. (Ephes. 1:14.) This is the case of all believers. They all have the Spirit.

Let it be distinctly understood that he who has not the Spirit has not Christ. He who has not Christ has no pardon of his sins—no peace with God—no title to heaven—no well-grounded hope of being saved. His religion is like the house built on the sand. It may look well in fine weather. It may satisfy him in the time of health and prosperity. But when the flood rises, and the wind blows—when sickness and trouble come up against him, it will fall and bury him under its ruins. He lives without a good hope, and without a good hope he dies. He will rise again only to be miserable. He will stand in the judgment only to be condemned; he will see saints and angels looking on, and remember he might have been among them—but too late; he will see lost myriads around him, and find they cannot comfort him—but too late. This will be the end of the man who thinks to reach heaven without the Spirit.

Settle these things down in your memory, and let them never be forgotten. Are they not worth remembering? No Holy Spirit in you—no part in Christ! No part in Christ—no forgiveness of sins! No forgiveness of sins—no peace with God! No peace with God—no title to heaven! No title to heaven—no admission into heaven! No admission into heaven—and what then? Yes—what then? You may well ask. Where will you flee? Which way will you turn? To what refuge will you run? There is none at all. There remains nothing but hell. Not admitted into heaven--you must sink at last into hell.

I ask every reader of this paper to mark well what I say. Perhaps it startles you—but may it not be good for you to be startled? Have I told you anything more than simple scriptural truth? Where is the defective link in the chain of reasoning you have heard? Where is the flaw in the argument? I believe in my conscience there is none. From not having the Spirit to being in hell, there is but a long flight of downward steps. Living without the Spirit, you are already on the top; dying without the Spirit, you will find your way to the bottom!

(b) Remember, for another thing, **if you have not the Spirit you have no holiness of heart, and no fitness for heaven.**

Heaven is the place to which all people hope to go after they die. It would be well for many if they considered calmly what kind of dwelling-place heaven is. It is the habitation of the King of kings, who is "of purer eyes than to behold iniquity," and it must needs be a holy place. It is a place into which Scripture tells us there shall enter in nothing "that defiles, neither whatever works abomination." (Rev. 21:27.) It is a place where there shall be nothing wicked, sinful, or sensual—nothing worldly, foolish, frivolous, or profane. There, let the covetous man remember, shall be no more money. There, let the pleasure seeker remember, shall be no more races, theaters, novel reading, or balls. There, let the drunkard and the gambler, remember, shall be no more strong drink, no more dice, no more betting, no more cards. The everlasting presence of God, saints, and angels—the perpetual doing of God's will—the complete absence of everything which God does not approve—these are the chief things which shall make up heaven. It shall be an eternal Sabbath day.

For this heaven we are all by nature utterly unfit. We have no capacity for enjoying its happiness. We have no taste for its blessings. We have no eye to see its beauty. We have no heart to feel its comforts. Instead of freedom, we would find it bondage. Instead of glorious liberty, we would find it constant constraint. Instead of a splendid palace, we would find it a gloomy prison. A fish on dry land, a sheep in the water, an eagle in a cage--would all feel more at ease and in their place than an unholy man in heaven. "Without holiness no man shall see the Lord." (Heb. 12:14.)

For this heaven it is the special office of the Holy Spirit to prepare men's souls. He alone can change the earthly heart, and purify the corrupt worldly affections of Adam's children. He alone can bring their minds into harmony with God, and tune them for the eternal company of saints, and angels, and Christ. He alone can make them love what God loves, and hate what God hates, and delight in God's presence. He alone can set the limbs of human nature, which were broken and dislocated by Adam's fall, and bring about a real unity between man's will and God's. And this He does for everyone that is saved. It is written of believers that they are "saved according to God's mercy," but it is "by the washing of regeneration, and renewing of the Holy Spirit." They are chosen unto salvation—but it is "through sanctification of the Spirit," as well as "belief of the truth." (Titus 3:5; 2 Thess. 2:13.)

Let this also be written down on the tablet of your memory. No entrance into heaven, without the Spirit first entering your heart upon earth! No admission into glory in the next life without previous sanctification in this life! No Holy Spirit in you in this world—then no heaven in the world to come! You would not be fit for it! You would not be ready for it! You would not like it! You would not enjoy it! There is much use made in the present day of the word "holy." Our ears are wearied with "holy church," and "holy baptism," and "holy days," and "holy water," and" holy services," and "holy priests." But one thing is a thousand times more important—and that is, to be made a really holy man by the Spirit. We must be made partakers of the Divine nature, while we are alive. We must "sow to the Spirit," if we would ever reap life everlasting. (2 Peter 1:4; Gal. 6:8.)

(c) Remember, for another thing, **if you have not the Spirit, you have no right to be considered a true Christian, and no will or power to become one.**

It requires little to make a 'Christian' according to the standard of the world. Only let a man be baptized and attend some place of worship, and the requirements of the world are satisfied. The man's belief may not be so intelligent as that of a Turk—he may be profoundly ignorant of the Bible. The man's practice may be no better than that of a heathen—many a respectable Hindu might put him to shame. But what of that? He is an Englishman! He has been baptized! He goes to church or chapel, and behaves decently when there! What more would you have? If you do not call him a Christian you are thought very uncharitable!

But it takes a great deal more than this to make a man a real Christian according to the standard of the Bible. It requires the cooperation of all the Three Persons of the Blessed Trinity. The election of God the Father—the blood and intercession of God the Son—the sanctification of God the Spirit—must all meet together on the soul that is to be saved. Father, Son, and Holy Spirit must unite to work the work of making any child of Adam a true Christian.

This is a deep subject, and one that must be handled with reverence. But where the Bible speaks with decision, there we may also speak with decision; and the words of the Bible have no meaning if the work of the Holy Spirit be not just as needful in order to make a man a true Christian, as the work of the Father or the work of the Son. "No man," we are told, "can say that Jesus is the Lord—but by the Holy Spirit." (1 Cor. 12:3.) True Christians, we are taught in Scripture, are "born of the Spirit." They live in the Spirit; they are led by the Spirit; by the Spirit they mortify the deeds of the body; by one Spirit they have access through Jesus unto the Father. Their graces are all the fruit of the Spirit; they are the temple of the Holy Spirit; they are a habitation of God through the Spirit; they walk after the Spirit; they are strengthened by the Spirit. Through the Spirit they wait for the hope of righteousness by faith. (John 3:6; Gal. 5:25; Rom. 8:13, 14; Eph. 2:18; Gal. 5:22; 1 Cor. 6:19; Eph. 2:22; Rom. 8:4; Eph. 3:16; Gal. 5:5.) These are plain Scriptural expressions. Who will dare to gainsay them?

The truth is that the deep corruption of human nature would make salvation impossible if it were not for the work of the Spirit. Without Him the Father's love and the Son's redemption are set before us in vain. The Spirit must reveal them, the Spirit must apply them, or else we are lost souls!

Nothing less than the power of Him who moved on the face of the waters in the day of creation can ever raise us from our low estate. He who said, "Let there be light, and there was light," must speak the word before anyone of us will ever rise to newness of life. He who came down on the day of Pentecost, must come down on our poor dead souls, before they will ever see the kingdom of God. Mercies and afflictions may move the surface of our hearts—but they alone will never reach the inner man. Sacraments, and services, and sermons may produce outward formality, and clothe us with a 'skin of religion'—but there will be no life. Ministers may make communicants, and fill churches with regular worshipers—the almighty power of the Holy Spirit alone can make true Christians, and fill heaven with glorified saints.

Let this also be written in your memory, and never forgotten. No Holy Spirit—no true Christianity! You must have the Spirit in you, as well as Christ for you--if you are ever to be saved. God must be your loving Father, Jesus must be your known Redeemer, the Holy Spirit must be your felt Sanctifier, or else it will be better for you never to have been born!

I press the subject on the serious consideration of all who read these pages. I trust I have said enough to show you that it is of vital importance to your soul to "have the Spirit." This is no abstruse and mysterious point of divinity; it is no nice question of which the solution matters little one way or another. It is a subject in which is bound up the everlasting peace of your soul.

You may not like the tidings. You may call it wild enthusiasm, or fanaticism, or extravagance. I take my stand on the plain teaching of the Bible. I say that God must dwell in your heart by the Spirit on earth--or you will never dwell with God in heaven.

"Ah," you may say, "I do not know much about it. I trust God will be merciful. I hope I shall go to heaven after all." I answer, No man ever yet tasted of Christ's mercy who did not also receive of His Spirit. No man was ever justified who was not also sanctified. No man ever went to heaven who was not led there by the Spirit.

II. Let me, in the second place, point out the great general rule and principle by which the question may be decided, whether we have the Spirit.

I can quite understand that the idea of knowing whether we "have the Spirit" is disagreeable to many minds. I am not ignorant of the objections which Satan at once stirs up in the natural heart. "It is impossible to know it," says one person, "it is a deep thing, and beyond our reach." "It is too mysterious a thing to inquire into," says another, "we must be content to leave the subject in uncertainty." "It is wrong to pretend to know anything about it," says a third, "we were never meant to look into such questions. It is only fit for enthusiasts and fanatics to talk of having the Spirit." I hear such objections without being moved by them. I say that it can be known whether a man has the Spirit. It can be known—it may be known, it ought to be known. It needs no vision from heaven, no revelation from an angel to discern it; it needs nothing but calm inquiry by the light of God's Word. Let us enter upon that inquiry.

All people have not the Holy Spirit. I regard the doctrine of an 'inward spiritual light enjoyed by all mankind' as an unscriptural delusion. I believe the modern notion of universal salvation to be a baseless dream. Without controversy, God has not left Himself without a witness in the heart of fallen man. He has left in every mind sufficient knowledge of right and wrong to make all people responsible and accountable. He has given to every child of Adam a conscience—but He has not given to every child of Adam the Holy Spirit. A man may have good wishes like Balaam, do many things like Herod, be almost persuaded like Agrippa, and tremble like Felix, and yet be as utterly destitute of the grace of the Spirit as these people were. Paul tells us that before conversion people may "know God" in a certain sense, and have "thoughts accusing or ex-cusing one another." But he also tells us that before conversion people are "without God" and "without Christ," have "no hope," and are "darkness" itself. (Rom. 1:21; 2:15; Eph. 2:12; 5:8.) The Lord Jesus Himself says of the Spirit, "The world sees Him not, neither knows Him—but you know Him, for He dwells with you, and shall be in you." (John 14:17.)

All members of Churches and baptized people have not the Spirit. I see no ground in Scripture for saying that every man who receives baptism receives the Holy Spirit, and that we ought to regard him as born of the Spirit. I dare not tell baptized people that they all have the Spirit, and that they only need "stir up the gift of God" within them in order to be saved. I see, on the contrary, that Jude speaks of members of the visible Church in his day as "not having the Spirit." Some of them probably had been baptized by the hands of apostles, and admitted into full communion with the professing Church. No matter! they "had not the Spirit." (Jude 19.)

It is vain to attempt to evade the power of this single expression. It teaches plainly that "having the Spirit "is not the lot of every man, and not the portion of every member of the visible Church of Christ. It shows the necessity of finding out some general rule and principle by which the presence of the Spirit in a man may be ascertained. He does not dwell in everyone. Baptism and churchmanship are no proofs of His presence. How, then, shall I know whether a man has the Spirit?

The presence of the Spirit in a man's soul can only be known by the effects which He produces. The fruits He causes to be brought forth in a man's heart and life, are the only evidence which can be depended on. A man's faith, a man's opinions, and a man's practice, are the witnesses we must examine, if we would find out whether a man has the Spirit. This is the rule of the Lord Jesus, "Every tree is known by his own fruit." (Luke 6:44.)

The effects which the Holy Spirit produces may always be seen. The man of the world may not understand them—they may in many cases be feeble and indistinct; but where the Spirit is, He will not be hidden. He is not idle when He enters the heart. He does not lie still. He does not sleep. He will make His presence known. He will shine out little by little through the windows of a man's daily habits and conversation, and manifest to the world that He is in him. A dormant, torpid, silent indwelling of the Spirit is a notion that pleases the minds of many. It is a notion for which I see no authority in the Word of God. I hold entirely with the Homily for Whit-Sunday, "As the tree is known by his fruit, so is also the Holy Spirit."

In whoever I see the effects and fruits of the Spirit, in that man I see one who has the Spirit. I believe it to be not only charitable to think so—but presumption to doubt it. I do not expect to behold the Holy Spirit with my bodily eyes, or to touch Him with my hands. But I need no angel to come down to show me where He dwells. I need no vision from heaven to tell me where I may find Him. Only show me a man in whom the fruits of the Spirit are to be seen, and I see one who "has the Spirit." I will not doubt the inward presence of the almighty cause, when I see the outward fact of an evident effect.

Can I see the **wind** on a stormy day? I cannot—but I can see the effects of its force and power. When I see the clouds driven before it, and the trees bending under it—when I hear it whistling through doors and windows, or howling round the chimney tops, I do not for a moment doubt its existence. I say, "There is a wind." Just so it is with the presence of the Spirit in the soul.

Can I see the dew of heaven as it falls on a summer evening? I cannot. It comes down softly and gently, noiseless and imperceptible. But when I go forth in the morning after a cloudless night, and see every leaf sparkling with moisture, and feel every blade of grass damp and wet, I say at once, "There has been a dew." Just so it is with the presence of the Spirit in the soul.

Can I see the hand of the sower when I walk through the corn fields in the month of July? I cannot. I see nothing but millions of ears rich with grain, and bending to the ground with ripeness—but do I suppose that harvest came by chance, and grew of itself? I suppose nothing of the kind. I know when I see those corn fields that the plough and the harrow were at work one day, and that a hand has been there which sowed the seed. Just so it is with the work of the Spirit in the soul.

Can I see the magnetism in the compass-needle? I cannot. It acts in a hidden mysterious way—but when I see that little piece of iron always turning to the north, I know at once that it is under the secret influence of magnetic power. Just so it is with the work of the Spirit in the soul.

Can I see the mainspring of my watch when I look upon its face? I cannot. But when I see the fingers going round and telling the hours and minutes of the day in regular succession, I do not doubt the mainspring's existence. Just so it is with the work of the Spirit.

Can I see the steersman of the homeward-bound ship, when she first comes in sight, and her sails whiten on the horizon? I cannot. But when I stand on the pier-head and see that ship working her course over the sea towards the harbor's mouth, like a thing of life, I know well there is one at the helm who guides her movements. Just so it is with the work of the Spirit.

I charge all my readers to remember this. **Establish it as a settled principle in your mind, that if the Holy Spirit really is in a person, it will be seen in the effects He produces on his heart and life.**

Beware of supposing that a man may have the Spirit when there is no outward evidence of His presence in the soul. It is a dangerous and unscriptural delusion to think so. We must never lose sight of the broad principles laid down for us in Scripture, "If we say that we have fellowship with Him, and walk in darkness, we lie, and do not the truth." "In this the children of God are manifest and the children of the devil—whoever does not righteousness is not of God." (1 John 1:6; 3:10.)

You have heard, I doubt not, of a wretched class of professing Christians called Antinomians. They are people who boast of having a saving interest in Christ, and say they are pardoned and forgiven, while at the same time they live in willful sin and open breach of God's commandments. I dare say that such people are miserably deceived. They are going down to hell with a lie in their right hand! The true believer in Christ is "dead to sin." Every person who has a real hope in Christ "purifies himself even as He is pure." (1 John 3:3.)

But I will tell you of a delusion quite as dangerous as that of the Antinomians, and far more specious. That delusion is—to flatter yourself you have the Spirit dwelling in your heart, while there are no fruits of the Spirit to be seen in your life. I firmly believe that this delusion is ruining thousands, as surely as Antinomianism. It is just as perilous to dishonor the Holy Spirit, as it is to dishonor Christ. It is just as offensive to God to pretend to an interest in the work of the Spirit, as it is to pretend to an interest in the work of Christ.

Once for all, I charge my readers to remember that the effects which the Spirit produces are the only trustworthy evidences of His presence. To talk of the Holy Spirit dwelling in you and yet being unseen in your life, is wild work indeed. It confounds the first principles of the Gospel—it confounds light and darkness—nature and grace—conversion and unconversion—faith and unbelief—the children of God and the children of the devil.

There is only one safe position in this matter. There is only one safe answer to the question, "How shall we decide who have the Spirit?" We must take our stand on the old principle laid down by our Lord Jesus Christ, "By their fruits you shall know them." (Matt. 7:20.) Where the Spirit is there will be fruit—he who has no fruit of the Spirit has not the Spirit. A work of the Spirit unfelt, unseen, inoperative, is a great delusion. Where the Spirit really is He will be felt, seen, and known.

III. Let me, in the last place, describe the particular effects which the Spirit produces on the souls in which He dwells.

I regard this part of the subject as the most important of all. Hitherto I have spoken generally of the great leading principles which must guide us in inquiring about the work of the Holy Spirit. I must now come closer, and speak of the special marks by which the presence of the Holy Spirit in any individual heart may be discerned. Happily, with the Bible for our light, these marks are not hard to find out.

Some things I wish to premise before entering fully into the subject. It is needful in order to clear the way.

(a) I grant freely that there are some deep mysteries about the work of the Spirit. I cannot explain the manner of His coming into the heart. "The wind blows where it wills, and you hear the sound thereof—but cannot tell whence it comes and where it goes—so is everyone that is born of the Spirit." (John 3:8.) I cannot explain why He comes into one heart and not into another—why He condescends to dwell in this man and not in that. I only know that so it is. He acts as a sovereign. To use the words of the Church Catechism, He sanctifies "the elect people of God." But I remember also that I cannot explain why I was born in Christian England, and not in heathen Africa. I am satisfied to believe that all God's work is well done. It is enough for me to be in the King's court, without being of the King's counsel.

(b) I grant freely that there are great diversities in the operations by which the Spirit carries on His work in men's souls. There are differences in the **ages** at which He begins to enter the heart. With some He begins young, as with John the Baptist and Timothy—with some he begins old, as with Manasseh and Zaccheus. There are differences in the feelings which He first stirs up in the heart. He leads some by strong terror and alarm, like the jailer at Philippi. He leads some by gently opening their hearts to receive the truth, as Lydia. There are differences in the time occupied in effecting this complete change of character. With some the change is immediate and sudden, as it was with Saul when he journeyed to Damascus—with others it is gradual and slow, as it was with Nicodemus the Pharisee. There are differences in the instruments He uses in first awakening the soul from its natural death. With some He uses a sermon, with others the Bible, with others a tract, with others a friend's advice, with others a sickness or affliction, with others no one particular thing that can be distinctly traced. All this is most important to understand. To require all people to be squared down to one kind of experience is a most grievous mistake!

(c) I grant freely that the beginnings of the Spirit's work are often small and imperceptible. The seed from which the spiritual character is formed, is often very minute at first. The fountain-head of the spiritual life, like that of many a mighty river, is frequently at its outset, only a little trickling stream. The beginnings therefore of the Spirit's work in a soul are generally overlooked by the world—very frequently not duly valued and encouraged by other Christians—and almost without exception thoroughly misunderstood by the soul itself which is the subject of them. Let that never be forgotten. The man in whom the Spirit begins to work is never hardly aware, until long afterwards, that his state of mind about the time of his conversion arose from the entrance of the Holy Spirit.

But still, after all these concessions and allowances, there are certain great leading effects which the Spirit produces on the soul in which He dwells, which are always one and the same. Those who have the Spirit may be led at first by different paths—but they are always brought, sooner or later, into one and the same narrow way. Their leading opinions of Gospel truth are the same; their leading desires are the same; their general walk is the same. They may differ from one another widely in their natural character—but their spiritual character, in its main features, is always one. The Holy Spirit always produces one general kind of effects. Shades and varieties there are no doubt in the experience of those on whose hearts He works—but the general outline of their faith and life is always the same.

What then are these general effects which the Spirit always produces on those who really have Him? **What are the marks of His presence in the soul?** This is the question which now remains to be considered. Let us try to set down these marks in order.

1. All who have the Spirit are quickened by Him, and made spiritually alive. He is called in Scripture, "The Spirit of life." (Rom. 8:3.) "It is the Spirit," says our Lord Jesus Christ, "who quickens." (John 6:63.) We are all by nature dead in trespasses and sins. We have neither feeling nor interest about true religion. We have neither faith, nor hope, nor fear, nor love. Our hearts are in a state of torpor; they are compared in Scripture to a stone. We may be alive about money, learning, politics, or pleasure—but we are dead towards God. All this is changed when the

Spirit comes into the heart. He raises us from this state of death, and makes us new creatures. He awakens the conscience, and inclines the will towards God. He causes old things to pass away, and all things to become new. He gives us a new heart; He makes us put off the old man, and put on the new. He blows the trumpet in the ear of our slumbering faculties, and sends us forth to walk the world as if we were new beings.

How unlike was Lazarus shut up in the silent tomb, to Lazarus coming forth at our Lord's command! How unlike was Jairus' daughter lying cold on her bed amidst weeping friends, to Jairus' daughter rising and speaking to her mother as she was accustomed to do! Just as unlike is the man in whom the Spirit dwells to what he was before the Spirit came into him.

I appeal to every thinking reader. Can he whose heart is manifestly full of everything but God--hard, cold, and insensible—can he be said to "have the Spirit"? Judge for yourself.

2. All who have the Spirit are taught by Him. He is called in Scripture, "The Spirit of wisdom and revelation." (Eph. 1:17.) It was the promise of the Lord Jesus, "He shall teach you all things." "He shall guide you into all truth." (John 14:26; 16:13.) We are all by nature ignorant of spiritual truth. "The natural man receives not the things of the Spirit of God—they are foolishness to him." (1 Cor. 2:14.) Our eyes are blinded. We neither know God, nor Christ, nor ourselves, nor the world, nor sin, nor heaven, nor hell, as we ought. We see everything under false colors. The Spirit alters entirely this state of things. He opens the eyes of our understandings. He illumines us; He calls us out of darkness into marvelous light. He takes away the veil. He shines into our hearts, and makes us see things as they really are! No wonder that all true Christians are so remarkably agreed upon the essentials of true religion! The reason is that they have all learned in one school—the school of the Holy Spirit.

No wonder that true Christians can understand each other at once, and find common ground of fellowship! They have been taught the same language, by One whose lessons are never forgotten.

I appeal again to every thinking reader. Can he who is ignorant of the leading doctrines of the Gospel, and blind to his own state—can he be said to "have the Spirit "? Judge for yourself

3. All who have the Spirit are led by Him to the scriptures. This is the instrument by which He specially works on the soul. The Word is called "the sword of the Spirit." Those who are born again are said to be "born by the Word." (Eph. 6:17; 1 Peter 1:23.) All Scripture was written under His inspiration—He never teaches anything which is not therein written. He causes the man in whom He dwells to "delight in the law of the Lord." (Psalm 1:2.) Just as the infant desires the milk which nature has provided for it, and refuses all other food--so does the soul which has the Spirit desire the sincere milk of the Word. Just as the Israelites fed on the manna in the wilderness, so are the children of God taught by the Holy Spirit to feed on the contents of the Bible.

I appeal again to every thinking reader. Can he who never reads the Bible, or only reads it formally—can he be said to have the Spirit? Judge for yourself.

4. All who have the Spirit are convinced by Him of Sin. This is an especial office which the Lord Jesus promised He should fulfill. "When He has come, He shall reprove the world of sin." (John 16:8.) He alone can open a man's eyes to the real extent of his guilt and corruption before God. He always does this when He comes into the soul. He puts us in our right place. He shows us the vileness of our own hearts, and makes us cry with the publican, "God be merciful to me a sinner!" He pulls down those proud, self-righteous, self-justifying notions with which we are all born, and makes us feel as we ought to feel, "I am a sinful man, and I deserve to be in hell!" Ministers may alarm us for a little season; sickness may break the ice on our hearts; but the ice will soon freeze again if it is not thawed by the breath of the Spirit! Convictions not wrought by Him will pass away like the morning dew.

I appeal again to every thinking reader. Can the man who never feels the burden of his sins, and knows not what it is to be humbled by the thought of them—can he have the Spirit? Judge for yourself.

5. All who have the Spirit are led by Him to Christ for salvation. It is one special part of His office to "testify of Christ," to "take of the things of Christ, and to show them to us." (John 15:26; 16:15.) By nature we all think to work our own way to heaven—we fancy in our blindness that we can make our peace with God. From this miserable blindness the Spirit delivers us. He shows us that in ourselves we are lost and hopeless, and that Christ is the only door by which we can enter heaven and be saved. He teaches us that nothing but the blood of Jesus can atone for sin, and that through His mediation alone God can be just and the justifier of the ungodly. He reveals to us the exquisite fitness and suitableness to our souls of Christ's salvation. He unfolds to us the beauty of the glorious doctrine of justification by simple faith. He sheds abroad in our hearts that mighty love of God which is in Christ Jesus. Just as the dove flies to the well-known cleft of the rock, so does the soul of him who has the Spirit flee to Christ and rest on Him. (Rom. 5:5.)

I appeal again to every thinking reader. Can he who knows nothing of faith in Christ, be said to have the Spirit? Judge for yourself.

6. All who have the Spirit are by Him made Holy. He is" the Spirit of holiness." (Rom. 1:4.) When He dwells in people, He makes them follow after love, joy, peace, long-suffering, gentleness, meekness, faith, patience, temperance." He makes it natural to them, through their new "Divine nature," to count all God's precepts concerning all things to be right, and to "hate every false way." (2 Pet 1:4; Ps. 119:128.) Sin is no more pleasant to them—it is their sorrow when tempted by it; it is their shame when they are overtaken by it. Their desire is to be free from it altogether. Their happiest times are when they are enabled to walk most closely with God—their saddest times are when they are furthest off from Him.

I appeal again to every thinking reader. Can those who do not even pretend to live strictly according to God's will, be said to have the Spirit? Judge for yourself.

7. All who have the Spirit are spiritually minded. To use the words of the Apostle Paul, "those who live according to the flesh set their minds on the things of the flesh, but those who live according to the Spirit set their minds on the things of the Spirit." (Rom. 8:5.) The general tone, tenor, and bias of their minds is in favor of spiritual things. They do not serve God by fits and starts—but habitually. They may be drawn aside by strong temptations; but the general tendency of their lives, ways, tastes, thoughts and habits, is spiritual. You see it in the way they spend their leisure time, the company they love to keep, and their conduct in their own homes. And all is the result of the spiritual nature implanted in them by the Holy Spirit. Just as the caterpillar when it becomes a butterfly can no longer be content to crawl on earth—but will fly upwards and use its wings, so will the affections of the man who has the Spirit be ever reaching upwards toward God.

I appeal again to every thinking reader. Can those whose minds are wholly intent on the things of this world be said to have the Spirit? Judge for yourself.

8. All who have the Spirit feel a conflict within them, between the old nature and the new. The words of Paul are true, more or less, of all the children of God, "The flesh lusts against the Spirit, and the Spirit against the flesh--so that you cannot do the things that you would."

(Gal. 5:17.) They feel a holy principle within their bosoms, which makes them delight in the law of God—but they feel another principle within, striving hard for the mastery, and struggling to drag them downwards and backwards. Some feel this conflict more than others—but all who have the Spirit are acquainted with it; and it is a token for good. It is a proof that the 'strong man armed' no longer *reigns* within, as he once did, with undisputed sway. The presence of the Holy Spirit may be known by inward warfare as well as by inward peace. He who has been taught to rest and hope in Christ, will always be one who fights and wars with sin.

I appeal again to every thinking reader. Can he who knows nothing of inward conflict, and is a servant to sin, the world, and his own self-will, can he be said to have the Spirit? Judge for yourself.

9. All who have the Spirit love others who have the Spirit. It is written of them by John, "We know that we have passed from death to life, because we love the brethren." (1 John 3:14.) The more they see of the Holy Spirit in anyone, the more dear he is to them. They regard him as a member of the same family, a child of the same Father, a subject of the same King, and a fellow-traveler with themselves in a foreign country towards the same father-land. It is the glory of the Spirit to bring back something of that brotherly love, which sin has so miserably chased out of the world. He makes people love one another for reasons which to the natural man are foolishness—for the sake of a common Savior, a common faith, a common service on earth, and the hope of a common home. He raises up friendships independent of blood, marriage, interest, business, or any worldly motive. He unites people by making them feel they are united to one great center, Jesus Christ.

I appeal again to every thinking reader. Can he who finds no pleasure in the company of spiritually-minded people, or even sneers at them as saints—can he be said to have the Spirit? Judge for yourself.

10. Finally, all who have the Spirit are taught by Him to pray.
He is called in Scripture, "The Spirit of grace and supplication." (Zech. 12:10.) The elect of God are said to "cry to Him night and day." (Luke 18:7.) They cannot help it—their prayers may be poor, and weak, and wandering—but pray they must; something within them tells them they must speak with God and lay their needs before Him. Just as the infant will cry when it feels pain or hunger, because it is its nature, so will the new nature implanted by the Holy Spirit oblige a man to pray. He has the Spirit of adoption, and he must cry, "Abba, Father." (Gal. 4:6.)

Once more I appeal to every thinking reader. Can the man who never prays at all, or is content with saying a few formal heartless words, can he be said to have the Spirit? For the last time I say, Judge for yourself.

Such are the marks and signs by which I believe the presence of the Holy Spirit in a man may be discerned. I have set them down fairly as they appear to me to be laid before us in the Scriptures. I have endeavored to exaggerate nothing, and to keep back nothing. I believe there are no true Christians in whom these marks may not be found. Some of them, no doubt, stand out more prominently in some, and others in others. My own experience is distinct and decided—that I never saw a truly godly person, even of the poorest and humblest classes, in whom, on close observation, these marks might not be discovered.

I believe that marks such as these are the only safe evidence that we are traveling in the way that leads to everlasting life. I charge everyone who desires to make his calling and election sure, to see that these marks are his own. There are high-flying professors of religion, I know, who despise the mention of "marks," and call them "legal." I care nothing for their being called legal, so long as I am satisfied they are scriptural. And, with the Bible before me, I give my opinion confidently, that he who is without these marks is without the Spirit of God.

Show me a man who has these marks, and I acknowledge him as a child of God. He may be poor and lowly in this world; he may be vile in his own eyes, and often doubt of his own salvation. But he has that within him which only comes from above, and will never be destroyed, even the work of the Holy Spirit. God is his, Christ is his. His name is already written in the book of life, and before long heaven will be his own.

Show me a man in whom these marks are not to be found, and I dare not acknowledge him to be a true Christian. I dare not as an honest man; I dare not as a lover of his soul; I dare not as a reader of the Bible. He may make a great religious profession; he may be learned, high in the world, and moral in his life. It is all nothing if he has not the Holy Spirit. He is without God, without Christ, without solid hope, and, unless he changes, will at length be without heaven.

And now let me finish this paper by a few **practical remarks** which arise naturally out of the matter which it contains.

(a) Would you know, first of all, what is your own immediate duty? Listen, and I will tell you.

You ought to examine yourself calmly about the subject which I have been trying to set before you. You ought to ask yourself seriously how the doctrine of the Holy Spirit affects your soul. Look away, I beseech you, for a few minutes, to higher things than the things of earth, and more important things than the things of time. Bear with me, while I ask you a plain question. I ask it solemnly and affectionately, as one who desires your salvation—Have you the Spirit?

Remember, I do not ask whether you think all I have been saying is true, and right, and good. I ask whether you yourself, who are reading these lines--have within you the Holy Spirit?

Remember, I do not ask whether you believe that the Holy Spirit is given to the Church of Christ, and that all who belong to the Church are within reach of His operations. I ask whether you yourself have the Spirit in your own heart?

Remember, I do not ask whether you sometimes feel strivings of conscience, and good desires flitting about within you. I ask whether you have really experienced the quickening and reviving work of the Spirit upon your heart?

Remember, I do not ask you to tell me the day or month when the Spirit began His work in you. It is enough for me if fruit trees bear fruit, without inquiring the precise time when they were planted. But I do ask--Are you bringing forth any fruits of the Spirit?

Remember, I do not ask whether you are a perfect person, and never feel anything evil within. But I do ask, gravely and seriously, whether you have about your heart and life the marks of the Spirit?

I hope you will not tell me you do not know what the marks of the Spirit are. I have described them plainly. I now repeat them briefly, and press them on your attention.

1. The Spirit quickens men's hearts.

2. The Spirit teaches men's minds.

3. The Spirit leads to the Word.

4. The Spirit convinces of sin.

5. The Spirit draws to Christ.

6. The Spirit sanctifies.

7. The Spirit makes people spiritually minded.

8. The Spirit produces inward conflict.

9. The Spirit makes people love the brethren.

10. The Spirit teaches to pray.

These are the great marks of the Holy Spirit's presence. Put the question to your conscience like a man—Has the Spirit done anything of this kind for your soul?

I charge you not to let many days pass away without trying to answer my question. I summon you, as a faithful watchman knocking at the door of your heart, to bring the matter to an outcome. We live in an old, worn-out, sin-laden world. Who can tell what "a day may bring forth?" Who shall live to see another year? Have you the Spirit? (Prov. 27:1.)

(b) Would you know, in the next place, what is the grand defect of the Christianity of our times? Listen to me, and I will tell you.

The grand defect I speak of is simply this—that the Christianity of many people is not real Christianity at all. I know that such an opinion sounds hard and shockingly uncharitable. I cannot help that—I am satisfied that it is sadly true. I only want people's Christianity to be that of the Bible; but I doubt exceedingly, in many cases, whether it is so.

There are multitudes of English people, I believe, who go to church or chapel every Sunday merely as a form. Their fathers or mothers went, and so they go; it is the fashion of the country to go, and so they go; it is the custom to attend a religious service and hear a sermon, and so they go. But as to real, vital, saving religion--they neither know nor care anything about it. They can give no account of the distinctive doctrines of the

Gospel. Justification, and regeneration, and sanctification, are "words and names" which they cannot explain. They may have a sort of vague idea that they ought to go to the Lord's Table, and may be able to say a few vague words about Christ—but they have no intelligent notion of the way of salvation. As to the Holy Spirit, they can scarcely say more about Him than that they have heard His name.

Now, if any reader of this paper is conscious that his religion is such as I have described, I will only warn him affectionately to remember that such religion is utterly useless. It will neither save, comfort, satisfy, nor sanctify his soul. And the plain advice I give him is to change it for something better without delay. Remember my words. It will not do at the last.

(c) Would you know, in the next place, one truth in the Gospel about which we need to be specially jealous in this day. Listen, and I will tell you.

The truth which I have in view is the truth about the work of the Holy Spirit. All truth no doubt is constantly assailed by Satan. I have no desire for a moment to exaggerate the office of the Spirit—and to exalt Him above the Sun and Center of the Gospel—Jesus Christ. But I do believe that, next to the priestly office of Christ, no truth in the present day is so frequently lost sight of, and so deceitfully assailed, as the work of the Spirit. Some injure it by ignorant neglect—their talk is all about Christ. They can tell you something about "the Savior;" but if you ask them about that inward work of the Spirit which all who really know the Savior experience, they have not a word to say.

Some injure the work of the Spirit by taking it all for granted. Membership of the Church, participation of the Sacraments, become their substitutes for conversion and spiritual regeneration. Some injure the work of the Spirit by confounding it with the action of natural conscience. According to this low view, none but the most hardened and degraded of mankind are destitute of the Holy Spirit. Against all such departures from the truth let us watch and be on our guard. Let us beware of leaving the proportion of Gospel statements. Let one of our chief watchwords in the present day be—**No salvation without the inward work of the Spirit! No inward work of the Holy Spirit unless it can be seen, felt, and known! No saving work of the Spirit which does not show itself in repentance towards God, and living faith towards Jesus Christ!**

(d) Would you know, in the next place, the reason why we, who are ministers of the Gospel, never despair of anyone who hears us so long as he lives? Listen, and I will tell you.

We never despair, because we believe the power of the Holy Spirit. We might well despair when we look at our own performances—we are often sick of ourselves! We might well despair when we look at some who belong to our congregations—they seem as hard and insensible as the nether mill-stone. But we remember the Holy Spirit, and what He has done; we remember the Holy Spirit, and consider that He has not changed. He can come down like fire and melt the hardest hearts! He can convert the worst man or woman among our hearers, and mold their whole character into a new shape. And so we preach on. We hope, because of the Holy Spirit. Oh, that our hearers would understand that the progress of true religion depends "not on might or on power," but on the Lord's Spirit! Oh, that many of them would learn to lean less on ministers, and to pray more for the Holy Spirit! Oh, that all would learn to expect less from schools, and tracts, and ecclesiastical machinery, and, while using all means diligently, would seek more earnestly for the outpouring of the Spirit. (Zech. 4:6.)

(e) Would you know, in the next place, what you ought to do, if your conscience tells you you have not the Spirit? Listen, and I will tell you.

If you have not the Spirit, you ought to go at once to the Lord Jesus Christ in prayer, and beseech Him to have mercy on you, and send you the Spirit. I have not the slightest sympathy with those who tell people to pray for the Holy Spirit in the first place, in order that they may go to Christ in the second place. I see no warrant of Scripture for saying so. I only see that if people feel they are needy, perishing sinners, they ought to apply first and foremost, straight and direct, to Jesus Christ. I see that He Himself says, "If any man thirsts, let him come unto Me and drink." (John 7:37.) I know that it is written, "He has received gifts for men, even for the rebellious, that the Lord God might dwell among them." (Psal. 68:18.) I know it is His special office to baptize with the Holy Spirit, and that "in Him all fullness dwells." I dare not pretend to be more systematic than the Bible. I believe that Christ is the meeting place between God and the soul, and my first advice to anyone who wants the Spirit must always be, "Go to Jesus, and tell your need to Him!" (Col. 1:19.)

Furthermore I would say, if you have not the Spirit, you must be diligent in attending those means of grace through which the Spirit works. You must regularly hear that Word, which is His sword; you must habitually attend those assemblies where His presence is promised. You must, in short, be found in the way of the Spirit, if you want the Spirit to do you good. Blind Bartimeus would never have received sight had he sat lazily at home, and not come forth to sit by the wayside. Zaccheus might never have seen Jesus and become a son of Abraham, if he had not run before and climbed up into the sycamore tree. The Spirit is a loving and good Spirit. But he who despises means of grace resists the Holy Spirit.

Remember these two things. I firmly believe that no man ever acted honestly and perseveringly on these two pieces of advice who did not, sooner or later, have the Spirit.

(f) Would you know, in the next place, what you ought to do, if you stand in doubt about your own state, and cannot tell whether you have the Spirit? Listen, and I will tell you.

If you stand in doubt whether you have the Spirit, you ought to examine calmly whether your doubts are well-founded. There are many true believers, I fear, who are destitute of any firm *assurance* as to their own state—doubting is their life. I ask such people to take their Bibles down, and consider quietly the grounds of their concerns. I ask them to consider whence came their sense of sin, however feeble—their love to Christ, however faint—their desire after holiness, however weak—their pleasure in the company of God's people—their inclination to prayer and the Word? Whence came these things, I say? Did they come from your own heart? Surely not! Sinful human nature bears no such fruit. Did they come from the devil? Surely not! Satan does not wage war against Satan. Whence then, I repeat, did these things come? I warn you to beware lest you grieve the Holy Spirit by doubting the truth of His operations. I tell you it is high time for you to reflect whether you have not been expecting an 'inward perfection' which you had no right to expect, and at the same time thanklessly undervaluing a real work which the Holy Spirit has actually wrought in your souls.

A great statesman once said that if a foreigner visited England, for the first time, with his eyes bandaged and his ears open—hearing everything—but seeing nothing—he might well suppose that England was on the road to ruin; so many are the murmurings of the English people. And yet if that same foreigner came to England with his ears stopped and his eyes open—seeing everything and hearing nothing—he would probably suppose that England was the most wealthy and flourishing country in the world, so many are the signs of prosperity that he would see.

I am often disposed to apply this remark to the case of doubting Christians. If I believed all they say of themselves I would certainly think they were in a bad state. But when I see them living as they do—hungering and thirsting after righteousness, poor in spirit, desiring holiness, loving the name of Christ, keeping up habits of Bible reading and prayer—when I see these things I cease to be afraid. I trust my eyes more than my ears. I see manifest marks of the Spirit's presence, and I only grieve that they should refuse to see them themselves. I see the devil robbing them of their peace, by instilling these doubts into their minds, and I mourn that they should injure themselves by believing him. Some professors, without controversy, may well doubt whether they "have the Spirit," for they have no signs of grace about them. But many nurse up a habit of doubt in their minds for which they have no cause, and of which they ought to be ashamed.

(g) **Would you know, last of all, what you ought to do, if you really have the Spirit.** Listen to me, and I will tell you.

If you have the Spirit, seek to be "filled with the Spirit." (Ephes. 5:18.) Drink deep of the living waters. Do not be content with a little religion. Pray that the Spirit may fill every corner and chamber of your heart, and that not an inch of room may be left in it for the world and the devil.

If you have the Spirit, "grieve not the Spirit." (Ephes. 4:30.) It is easy for believers to weaken their sense of His presence, and deprive themselves of His comfort. Little sins not mortified, little bad habits of temper or of tongue not corrected, little compliances with the world, are all likely to offend the Holy Spirit. Oh, that believers would remember this! There is far more of "heaven on earth" to be enjoyed than many of them attain to—and why do they not attain to it? They do not watch sufficiently over

their daily ways, and so the Spirit's work is damped and hindered. The
Spirit must be a thoroughly sanctifying Spirit if He is to be a comforter
to your soul.

If you have the Spirit, labor to bring forth all the fruits of the Spirit.
"But the fruit of the Spirit is love, joy, peace, patience, kindness, goodness, faithfulness, gentleness, self-control; against such things there is no
law. And those who belong to Christ Jesus have crucified the flesh with
its passions and desires." (Galatians 5:22-24)

Read over the list which the Apostle has drawn out, and see that not
one of these fruits is neglected. Oh, that believers would seek for more
"love," and more "joy!" Then would they do more good to all people;
then would they feel happier themselves; then would they make religion
more beautiful in the eyes of the world!

I commend the things that I have written to the serious attention of
every reader of these pages. Let them not have been written in vain. Join
with me in praying that the Spirit may be poured out from on high with
more abundant influence than He has ever been yet. Pray that He may
be poured out on all believers, at home and abroad, that they may be
more united and more holy. Pray that He may be poured out on Jews,
Muhammadans, and Heathen, that many of them may be converted.

Pray that He may be poured out on Roman Catholics, and especially
in Italy and Ireland. Pray that He may be poured out on your own
country, and that it may be spared the judgments it deserves. Pray that
He may be poured out on all faithful ministers and missionaries, and that
their numbers may be increased an hundredfold. Pray, above all, that He
may be poured out, in abundant power, on your own soul--that if you
know not the truth, you may be taught to know it, and that if you know
it, you may know it better.

Chapter Six

The Power of the Holy Spirit

"Helmingham Series" tracts, not published since the 19th Century.

There is hope in the Gospel for any man, so long as he lives. There is infinite willingness in Christ to *pardon sin*. There is infinite power in the Holy Spirit *to change hearts*.

There are many diseases of the body which are incurable. The cleverest doctors cannot heal them. But, thank God! there are no incurable diseases of soul. All manner and quantity of sins can be washed away by Christ. The hardest and most wicked of hearts can be *changed*.

Reader, I say again, while there is life there is hope. The oldest, the vilest, the worst of sinners may be saved. Only let him come to Christ, confess his sin, and cry to Him for pardon,—only let him cast his soul on Christ, and he shall be cured. The Holy Spirit shall be sent down on his heart, according to Christ's promise, and he shall be changed by His Almighty power into a new creature.

I never despair of any one becoming a decided Christian, whatever he may have been in days gone by. I know how great the change is from death to life; I know the mountains of division that seem to stand between some men and heaven; I know the hardness, the prejudices, the desperate sinfulness of the natural heart; but I remember that God the Father made the glorious world out of nothing. I remember the voice of the Lord Jesus could reach Lazarus when four days dead, and recall him even from the grave; I remember the amazing victories the Spirit of God has won in every nation under heaven; I remember all this, and feel that I never need despair. Yes! those very persons who now seem most utterly dead in sins, may yet be raised to a new being, and walk before God in newness of life.

Why should it not be so? the Holy Spirit is a mighty, merciful, and loving Spirit. He turns away from no man because of his vileness. He passes by no one because his sins are black and scarlet.

There was nothing in the Corinthians that He should come down and quicken them. Paul reports of them that they were "fornicators, idolaters, adulterers, effeminate, thieves, covetous, drunkards, revilers, extortioners." "Such," he says, "were some of you." Yet even them the Spirit made alive. "Ye are washed," he writes, "ye are sanctified, ye are justified in the name of the Lord Jesus, and by the Spirit of our God" (1 Cor. vi. 9-11).

There was nothing in the Colossians that He should visit their hearts. Paul tells us that they walked in "fornication, uncleanliness, inordinate affection, evil concupiscence, and covetousness, which is idolatry." Yet them also the Spirit quickened. He made them "put off the old man with his deeds, and put on the new man, which is renewed in knowledge after the image of Him that created him" (Col. iii. 5-10).

There was nothing in Mary Magdalene that the Spirit should make her soul alive. Once she had been possessed with seven devils; time was, if report be true, she had been a woman proverbial for vileness and iniquity: yet even her the Spirit made a new creature,—separated her from her sins, —brought her to Christ,—made her last at the cross, and first at the tomb.

Never, never will the Spirit turn away from a soul because of its corruption. He never has done so;—He never will. It is His glory that He has purified the minds of the most impure, and made them temples for His own abode. He may yet take the worst of those who read this tract and make him a vessel of grace.

Why indeed should it not be so? The Spirit is an Almighty Spirit. He can change the stony heart into a heart of flesh; He can break the strongest bad habits like tow before the fire; He can make the most difficult things seem easy, and the mightiest objections melt away like snow in spring; He can cut the bars of brass, and throw the gates of prejudice wide open; He can fill up every valley, and make every rough place smooth. He has done it often, and He can do it again,

The Spirit can take a Jew,—the bitterest enemy of Christianity, the fiercest persecutor of true believers, the strongest stickler for Pharisaical notions, the most prejudiced opposer of Gospel doctrine,—and turn that man into an earnest preacher of the very faith he once destroyed. He has done it already.—He did it with the Apostle Paul.

The Spirit can take a Roman Catholic monk, brought up in the midst of Romish superstition,—trained from his infancy to believe false doctrine, and obey the Pope, —steeped to the eyes in error,—and make that man the clearest upholders of justification by faith the world ever saw; He has done so already.—He did it with Martin Luther.

The Spirit can take an English tinker, without learning, patronage, or money,—a man at one time notorious for nothing so much as blasphemy and swearing,—and make that man write a religious book, which shall stand unrivalled and unequalled in its way by any since the time of the

Apostles. He has done so already—He did it with John Bunyan, the author of "Pilgrim's Progress."

The Spirit can take a sailor, drenched in worldliness and sin,—a profligate captain of a slave ship,—and make that man amost successful minister of the Gospel; a writer of letters which are a store-house of experimental religion; and of hymns which are known and sung wherever English is spoken. He has done it already. —He did it with John Newton.

All this the Spirit has done, and much more, of which I cannot speak particularly. And the arm of the Spirit is not shortened: His power is not decayed. He is like the Lord Jesus,—the same yesterday, today, and forever. He is still doing wonders, and will do to the very end.

I shall not be surprised to hear, even in this life, that the hardest man I know has become softened, and the proudest has taken his place at the feet of Jesus as a weaned child.

I shall not be surprised to meet many on the right hand in the day of judgment, whom I shall leave, when I die, travelling in the broad way.

I never despair, because I believe the power of the Holy Ghost. We ministers might well despair, when we look at our own performances. We are often sick of ourselves. We might well despair when we look at some who belong to our congregations; they seem as hard and insensible as the nether mill-stone: but we remember the Holy Ghost, and what He has done. We remember the Holy Ghost, and consider that He has not changed. He can come down like fire and melt the hardest hearts; He can convert the worst man or woman among our hearers, and mould their whole character into a new shape. And so we preach on. We hope because of the Holy Ghost. Oh, that our hearts would understand that the progress of true religion depends not on might or on power, but on the Lord's Spirit! Oh, that many of them would learn to lean less on ministers, and to pray more for the Holy Spirit! Oh, that all would learn to expect less from schools, and tracts, and ecclesiastical machinery; and, while using all means diligently, would seek more earnestly for the outpouring of the Spirit.

Reader, do you feel the slightest drawing towards God?—the smallest concern about your immortal soul? Does your conscience tell you this day that you have not yet felt the Spirit's power, and do you want to know what to do? Listen, and I will tell you.

For one thing, you must go at once to the Lord Jesus Christ in prayer, and beseech Him to have mercy on you, and send you the Spirit. You must go direct to that open fountain of living waters, the Lord Jesus Christ, and you shall receive the Holy Ghost (John vii. 39). Begin at once to pray for the Holy Spirit. Think not you are shut up and cut off from hope: the Holy Ghost is promised to them that ask Him. His very name is the Spirit of Promise, and the Spirit of Life. Give Him no rest till He comes down and makes you a new heart. Cry mightily unto the Lord,—say unto Him, "Bless me, even me also: quicken me, and make me alive."

I dare not, for my part, send anxious souls to any one but Christ. I cannot hold with those who tell men to pray for the Holy Spirit in the first place, in order that they may go to Christ in the second place. I see no warrant of Scripture for saying so. I only see that if men feel they are needy, perishing sinners, they ought to apply, first and foremost, straight and direct to Jesus Christ. I see that He himself says, "If any man thirst, let him come unto Me and drink" (John vii. 37). I know that it is written, "He hath received gifts for men, yea for the rebellious also, that the Lord God might dwell among them" (Ps. lxviii. 18). I know it is His special office to baptize with the Holy Ghost, and that "in Him all fulness dwells." I dare not pretend to be more systematic than the Bible. I believe that Christ is the meeting-place between God and the soul: and my first advice to any one who wants the Spirit, must always be, "*go to Jesus, and tell your wants to Him.*"

For another thing, if you have not yet felt the converting power of the Spirit, you must be diligent in attending those means of grace through which the Spirit works. You must regularly hear that Word which is His sword; you must habitually attend those assemblies where His presence is promised; you must, in short, be found *in the way of the Spirit,* if you want the Spirit to do you good. Blind Bartimeus would never have received sight had he sat lazily at home, and not come forth to sit by the way-side. Zaccheus might never have seen Jesus, and become a son of Abraham, if he had not ran before and climbed up into the sycamore tree. The Spirit is a loving and good Spirit. *But he who despises means of grace, resists the Holy Ghost.*

Reader, remember these two things. I firmly believe that no man ever acted honestly and perseveringly on these two pieces of advice, who did not, sooner or later, have the Spirit, and find by experience that He is "mighty to save."

Chapter Seven

Teaching About the Holy Spirit

On the last day of the feast, the greatest day, Jesus stood up and shouted out, "If anyone is thirsty, let him come to me, and let the one who believes in me drink. Just as the scripture says, 'From within him will flow rivers of living water.'" (Now he said this about the Spirit, whom those who believed in him were going to receive, for the Spirit had not yet been given, because Jesus was not yet glorified.) - John 7:37-39

I t has been said that there are some passages in Scripture which deserve to be printed in letters of gold. Of such passages the verses before us form one. They contain one of those wide, full, free invitations to mankind, which make the Gospel of Christ so eminently the "good news of God." Let us see of what it consists.

We have, first, in these verses, *a case supposed.* The Lord Jesus says, "If any man thirst." These words no doubt were meant to have a spiritual meaning. The thirst before us is of a purely spiritual kind. It means anxiety of soul--conviction of sin--desire of pardon--longing after peace of conscience. When a man feels his sins, and wants forgiveness--is deeply sensible of his soul's need, and earnestly desires help and relief--then he is in that state of mind which our Lord had in view, when he said, "If any man thirst." The Jews who heard Peter preach on the day of Pentecost, and were "pierced in their hearts,"--the Philippian jailer who cried to Paul and Silas, "What must I do to be saved?" are both examples of what the expression means. In both cases there was "thirst."

Such thirst as this, unhappily, is known by few. All ought to feel it, and all would feel it if they were wise. Sinful, mortal, dying creatures as we all are, with souls that will one day be judged and spend eternity in heaven or hell, there lives not the man or woman on earth who ought not to "thirst" after salvation. And yet the many thirst after everything almost except salvation. Money, pleasure, honor, rank, self-indulgence--these are the things which they desire. There is no clearer proof of the fall of man, and the utter corruption of human nature, than the careless indifference of most people about their souls. No wonder the Bible calls the natural man "blind," and "asleep," and "dead," when so few can be found who are awake, alive, and athirst about salvation.

Happy are those who know something by experience of spiritual "thirst." The beginning of all true Christianity is to discover that we are guilty, empty, needy sinners. Until we know that we are lost, we are not in the way to be saved. The very first step toward heaven is to be thoroughly convinced that we deserve hell. That sense of sin which sometimes alarms a man and makes him think his own case desperate, is a good sign. It is in fact a symptom of spiritual life--"Blessed indeed are they which hunger and thirst after righteousness, for they shall be filled." (Matt. 5:6.)

We have, secondly, in these verses, *a remedy proposed.* The Lord Jesus says, "If any man thirst, let him come unto me and drink." He declares that He is the true fountain of life, the supplier of all spiritual necessities, the reliever of all spiritual needs. He invites all who feel the burden of sin heavy, to apply to Him, and proclaims Himself their helper.

Those words "let him come unto me," are few and very simple. But they settle a mighty question which all the wisdom of Greek and Roman philosophers could never settle; they show how man can have peace with God. They show that peace is to be had in Christ by trusting in Him as our mediator and substitute, in one word, by believing. To "come" to Christ is to believe on Him, and to "believe" on Him is to come. The remedy may seem a very simple one, too simple to be true. But there is no other remedy than this; and all the wisdom of the world can never find a flaw in it, or devise a better one.

To use this grand prescription of Christ is the secret of all saving Christianity. The saints of God in every age have been men and women who drank of this fountain by faith, and were relieved. They felt their guilt and emptiness, and thirsted for deliverance. They heard of a full supply of pardon, mercy, and grace in Christ crucified for all penitent believers. They believed the good news and acted upon it. They cast aside all confidence in their own goodness and worthiness, and came to Christ by faith as sinners. So coming they found relief. So coming daily they lived. So coming they died. Really to feel the sinfulness of sin and to thirst, and really to come to Christ and believe, are the two steps which lead to heaven. But they are mighty steps. Thousands are too proud and careless to take them. Few, alas! think, and still fewer believe.

We have, lastly, in these verses, *a promise held out.* The Lord Jesus says, "He that believes on me, from within him will flow rivers of living water." These words of course were meant to have a figurative sense. They have a double application. They teach, for one thing, that all who come to Christ by faith shall find in Him abundant satisfaction. They teach, for another thing, that believers shall not only have enough for the needs of their own souls, but shall also become fountains of blessings to others.

The fulfillment of the first part of the promise could be testified by thousands of living Christians in the present day. They would say, if their evidence could be collected, that when they came to Christ by faith, they found in Him more than they expected. They have tasted peace, and hope, and comfort, since they first believed, which, with all their doubts and fears, they would not exchange for anything in this world. They have found grace according to their need, and strength according to their days. In themselves and their own hearts they have often been disappointed; but they have never been disappointed in Christ.

The fulfillment of the other half of the promise will never be fully known until the judgment-day. That day alone shall reveal the amount of good that every believer is made the instrument of doing to others, from the very day of his conversion. Some do good while they live, by their tongues; like the Apostles and first preachers of the Gospel. Some do good when they are dying; like Stephen and the penitent thief, and our own martyred Reformers at the stake. Some do good long after they are dead, by their writings; like Baxter and Bunyan and M'Cheyne. But in one way or another, probably, almost all believers will be found to have been fountains of blessings. By word or by deed, by precept or by example, directly or indirectly, they are always leaving their marks on others. They know it not now; but they will find at last that it is true. Christ's saying shall be fulfilled.

Do we ourselves know anything of "coming to Christ?" This is the question that should arise in our hearts as we leave this passage. The worst of all states of soul is to be without feeling or concern about eternity--to be without "thirst." The greatest of all mistakes is to try to find relief in any other way than the one before us--the way of simply "coming to Christ." It is one thing to come to Christ's Church, Christ's ministers, and Christ's ordinances. It is quite another thing to come to Christ Himself. Happy is he who not only knows these things, but acts upon them!

Technical Notes:

37. On the last day, that great *day* of the feast, Jesus stood and cried, saying, If any man thirsts, let him come to me and drink. 38. He who believes on me, as the scripture has said, out of his belly shall flow rivers of living water. 39. (But this he spoke concerning the Spirit, whom those believing on him should receive; for the Holy Ghost was not yet *given*, because Jesus was not yet glorified.)37.--[*On the last day...feast.*] There seems to be in interval of three days between this verse and the preceding one. At any rate, it is certain that our Lord went to the temple and taught "about the midst of the feast." (v.14.) There seems no break from that point but a continuous narrative of teaching and argument up to this verse. There is, therefore, no account of what our Lord did during the three latter days of the feast. We can only conjecture that He taught on uninterrupted, and that a restraint was put by Divine interposition on His enemies so that they dared not interfere with Him.Whether this "last day of the feast" means the eighth day or the seventh is a question not decided.(1) Some, as Bengel and others, think it must be the seventh day, because in the account of the feast of tabernacles given by Moses there is no special mention of anything to be done on the eighth day (Lev. xxiii.33-43); while on each of the seven days of the feast there were special sacrifices appointed, a special reading of the law once every seven years, and also, according to the Jewish writers, a solemn drawing of water from the pool of Siloam to be poured on the altar in the temple.(2) Others,

as Lightfoot, Gill, Alford, Stier, Wordsworth, and Burgon, think it must be the eighth day, because in reality the feast could hardly be said to be finished till the end of the eighth day; and even in the account of the feast in Leviticus, it is said that the eighth day is to be "a holy convocation" and a "Sabbath." (Lev. xxiii.36 and 39.) The point is of no practical importance, but of the two opinions I incline to prefer the second one. The words seem to me to indicate that all the ceremonial of the feast was over, the last offerings had been made, and the people were on the point of dispersing to their respective homes when our Lord seized the opportunity and made the grand proclamation which immediately follows. It was a peculiarly typical occasion. The last feast of the year was concluding, and before it concluded our Lord proclaimed publicly the great truth which was the commencement of a new dispensation, and Himself as the end of all sacrifices and ceremonies. The objection that no drawing and pouring of water took place on the eighth day appears to me of no weight. That our Lord referred to it is highly probable. But I think He referred to it as a thing which the Jews had seen seven days running and remembered well. Now on the eighth day, when there was no water drawn, there seemed a peculiar fitness in His crying, "Come unto Me and drink. The water of life that I give may be drawn, though the feast is over."[*Jesus stood and cried.*] These words must mean that our Lord chose some high and prominent position where He could "stand" and be seen and heard by many persons at once. If, as we may suppose, the worshipers at the feast of tabernacles were just turning away from the last of its ceremonies, one can easily imagine that our Lord "stood" in some commanding position close by the entrance of the temple. When it is said that "He cried," it means that He lifted up His voice in a loud, and to Him, unusual manner in order to arrest attention, like a herald making a public proclamation.

[*If any man thirsts, let him come to Me and drink.*] These words can have but one meaning: they are a general invitation to all who are athirst about their souls to come to Christ in order to obtain relief. He declares Himself to be the fountain of life, the reliever of man's spiritual needs, the giver of satisfaction to weary consciences, the remover and pardoner of sins. He recommends all who feel their sins and want pardon to come to Him, and promises that they shall at once get what they want. The idea is precisely the same as that in Matt. xi.28, though the image employed is different.It is probable, as almost all commentators remark, that our Lord chose this figure and imagery because of the Jewish custom of drawing water from the pool of Siloam during the feast of tabernacles and carrying it in solemn procession to the temple. And it is thought that our Lord purposely refers to this ceremony of which the minds of many would doubtless be full. "Does anyone want true water of life, better than any water of Siloam? Let him come to Me and by faith draw out of Me living waters, even peace of conscience and pardon of sins." But is is fair to remember that this is only conjecture. This custom of drawing water from Siloam at the feast was a human invention, nowhere commanded in the law of Moses or even mentioned in the Old Testament; and it admits of doubt whether our Lord would have sanctioned it. Moreover, it is evident from John iv.10 and vi.35 that the figures of "water" and "thirst" were not infrequently used by our Lord. The figures, at any rate, were familiar to all Jews, from Isaiah lv.1. Some have thought that because the feast of tabernacles was specially intended to remind the Jews of their sojourn in the wilderness, our Lord had in view the miraculous supply of water from the rock which followed Israel everywhere, and that He wished the Jews to see in Him the fulfillment of that type, the true Rock. (1 Cor. x.4.) The idea is deserving of attention.The whole sentence is one of those golden sayings which ought to be dear to every true Christian, and is full of wide encouragement to all sinners who hear it. Its words deserve special attention. We should note *the breadth* of the invitation. It is for "any man." No matter who and what he may have been, no matter how bad and wicked his former life, the hand is held out and the offer made to him: "If any man thirsts, let him come." Let no man say that the Gospel is narrow in its offers. We should note *the persons* invited. They are those who "thirst." That expression is a figurative one, denoting the spiritual distress and anxiety which anyone feels when he discovers the value of his soul, the sinfulness of sin, and his own guilt. Such a one feels a burning desire for relief, of which the distressing sensation of "thirst," (a sensation familiar to all Eastern nations), is a most fitting emblem. No further qualification is named. There is no mention of repentance, amendment, preparation, conditions to fulfill, new heart to be got. One thing alone is named. Does a man "thirst"? Does he feel his sins and need of pardon? Then the Lord invites him. We should note *the simplicity* of the course prescribed to a thirsting sinner. It is simply, "Let him come unto Me." He has only to cast his soul on Christ, trust Him, lean on Him, believe on Him, commit his soul with all its burdens to Him, and that is enough. To trust Christ is to "come" to Christ. So "coming," Christ will supply all his need. So believing, he is at once forgiven, justified, and received into the number of God's children. (See John vi.35,37.)The expression "drink" is, of course, figurative, answering to the word "thirst." It means, "Let him freely take from Me everything that his soul needs—mercy, grace, pardon, peace, strength. I am the Fountain of Life. Let him use Me as such, and I shall be well pleased." We do not read of any prophet or apostle in the Bible who ever used such language as this and said to men, "Come unto me and drink." None surely could use it but one who knew that He was very God.

38.--[*He who believes on Me, etc.*] This verse is undoubtedly full of difficulties and has received very various interpretations. Not the least difficulty is about the connection in which the several expressions of the verse ought to be taken.(1) Some, as Stier, would connect "He who believes on Me" with the verb "drink" in the preceding verse. It would then run thus: "If any man thirst, let him come unto Me and let him drink who believes on Me." I cannot think this is a right view. For one thing, it would be a violent strain of all grammatical usage of the Greek language to interpret the words thus. For another thing, it would introduce doctrinal confusion. Our Lord's invitation was not made to him "who believes," but to him who is "athirst."(2) Some, as Chrysostom, Theophylact, Pellican, Heinsius, Gualter, DeDieu, Lightfoot, Trapp, and Henry, would connect "He who believes on Me" with the following words, "as the Scripture has said." It would then mean: "He who believes on Me after the manner that the Scripture bids him believe." I cannot think that this interpretation is correct. The expression "Believe as the Scripture has said," is a very strange and vague one and unlike anything else in the Bible.(3) Most commentators think that the words, "as the Scripture has said," must be taken in connection with those that follow, "out of his belly," etc. They think that our Lord did not mean to quote precisely any one text of Scripture, but only to give in His own words the general sense of several well-known texts. This, in spite of difficulties, I believe is the only satisfactory view. One difficulty, of a grammatical kind, arises from the expression "He who believes on Me" having no verb with which it is connected in the verse. This cannot be got over. It must be taken as a nominative absolute, and the sentence must be regarded as an elliptical sentence which we must fill up. Another difficulty arises from the fact that there is no text in the Old Testament Scriptures which at all answers to the quotation apparently given here.

This difficulty is undeniable, but not insuperable. As I have already said, our Lord did not intend to give an exact quotation but only the general substance of several Old Testament promises. Wordsworth thinks Matt. ii.23 a similar case. Jerome also maintains that frequently the inspired writers contented themselves with giving the sense and not the precise words of a quotation. (See also Eph. v.14.) Another difficulty arises as to the application of the words, "Out of his belly shall flow rivers of living water." Some, as Rupertus, Bengel, and Stier, would apply this to our Lord Himself and say that it means, "Out of Christ's belly shall flow rivers of living water." But it is a grave objection to this view that it totally disconnects the beginning of the verse from the end, makes the expression "He who believes on Me" even more elliptical than it needs to be, and throws the latter part of the verse in the form of a precise quotation of Scripture. I venture to think that the true interpretation of the verse is as follows:" He who believes on Me, or comes to Me by faith as his Savior, is the man out of whose belly shall flow rivers of living water, as the Scripture has said it should be." It is a strong argument in favor of this view that our Lord said to the Samaritan woman, that the water He could give would be in him who drank it "a well of water springing up into everlasting life." (John iv.14.) The full meaning of the promise is that every believer in Christ shall receive abundant satisfaction of his own spiritual needs; and not only that, but shall also become a source of blessing to others. From him instrumentally, by his word, work, and example, waters of life shall flow forth to the everlasting benefit of his fellowmen. He shall have enough for himself and shall be a blessing to others. The imagery of the figure used is still kept up, and "his belly" must stand for "his inner man." His heart being filled with Christ's gifts, shall overflow to others, and having received much shall give and impart much. The passages to which our Lord referred, and the substance of which He gives, are probably Isaiah xii.3, xxxv.6,7, xli.18, xliv.3, lv.1, lviii.11, Zech. xiv.8,16. Of these passages, our Lord gives the general sense but not the precise words. This is the view of Calvin, Beza, Grotius, Cocceius, Diodati, Lampe, and Scott. It is a curious, confirmatory fact that the Arabic and Syriac versions of the text both have the expression "Scripture" in the plural, "As the *Scriptures* have said." It is a curious fact which Bengel mentions, that the 14th chapter of Zechariah was read in public in the temple on the first day of the feast of tabernacles. If this is correct, we can hardly doubt that our Lord must have had this in mind when He used the expression "As the Scripture has said." It is as though He said, "As you have heard, for instance, during this very feast from the book of your prophet Zechariah." That almost every believer whose life is spared after he believes becomes a fountain of blessing and good to others, is a simple matter of fact which needs no illustration. A truly converted man always desires the conversion of others and labors to promote it. Even the thief on the cross, short as his life was after he repented, cared for his brother thief, and from the words he spoke have flowed "rivers of living water" over this sinful world for more than eighteen hundred years. He alone has been a fountain of blessing. Bloomfield quotes a Rabbinical sentence: "When a man turns to the Lord, he is like a fountain filled with living water, and rivers flow from him to men of all nations and tribes." The favorite notion of some, that our Lord in this place only referred to the miraculous gifts of the Holy Ghost to be given on the day of Pentecost, is an idea that does not commend itself to me at all. The thing before us is a thing promised to *every believer*. But the miraculous gifts were certainly not bestowed on *every* believer. Thousands were evidently converted through the Apostles' preaching who did not receive these gifts. Yet all received the Holy Ghost. Luther paraphrases this verse thus: "He who comes to Me shall be so furnished with the Holy Ghost that he shall not only be quickened and refreshed himself and delivered from thirst, but he shall also be a strong stone vessel from which the Holy Ghost in all His gifts shall flow to others—refreshing, comforting, and strengthening them even as he was refreshed by Me. So St. Peter on the day of Pentecost, by one sermon as by a rush of water, delivered three thousand men from the devil's kingdom, washing them in an hour from sin, death, and Satan." Hengstenberg, after quoting this, adds: "That was only the first exhibition of a glorious peculiarity which distinguishes the Church of the New Testament from the Church of the Old. She has a living impulse which will diffuse the life within her, even to the ends of the earth."39.--[*But this He spoke concerning the Spirit.*] This verse is one of those explanatory comments which are so common in St. John's Gospel. The opening words would be more literally rendered, "He spoke this concerning the Spirit."Let it be noted that here, at any rate, there can be no doubt that "water" does not mean "baptism," but the Holy Spirit. St. John himself says so in unmistakable language.[*Whom those believing on Him should receive.*] This means, "Whom believers in Him were about to receive." There is an inseparable connection between faith in Christ and receiving the Holy Ghost. If any man has faith, he has the Spirit. If any man has not the Spirit, he has no saving faith in Christ. The effectual work of the Second and Third Persons in the Trinity is never divided.Rupertus thinks that our Lord had specially in view that mighty outpouring of the Spirit on the Gentile world which was to take place after His own ascension into heaven, and the going forth of the Apostles into the world to preach the Gospel.[*For the Holy Ghost was not yet given, etc.*] This sentence means that the Holy Ghost was not yet poured out on believers in all His fullness, because our Lord had not yet finished His work by dying, rising again, and ascending into heaven for us. It was not till He was "glorified" by going up into heaven and taking His seat at the right hand of God that the Holy Ghost was sent down in full influence on the Church. Then was fulfilled Psalm lxviii.18--"You have ascended on high, You have led captivity captive; You have received gifts for man, yes, for the rebellious also, that the Lord God might dwell among them." Before our Lord died and rose again and ascended, the Holy Ghost was and had been from all eternity one with the Father and the Son, a distinct Person of equal power and authority, very and eternal God. But He had not revealed Himself so fully to those whose hearts He dwelt in as He did after the ascension; and He had not come down in person on the Gentile world or sent forth the Gospel to all mankind with rivers of blessing as He did when Paul and Barnabas were "sent forth by the Holy Ghost." (Acts xiii.4.) In a word, the dispensation of the Spirit had not yet begun. The expression "the Holy Ghost was not yet given" would be more literally rendered "the Holy Ghost was not." This cannot, of course, mean that the Holy Ghost did not exist and was in no sense present with believers in the Old Testament dispensation. On the contrary, the Spirit strove with the men of Noah's day, David spoke by the Holy Ghost, Isiah spoke of the Holy Spirit, and John the Baptist, now dead, was filled with the Holy Ghost from his mother's womb. (Gen. vi.4, Mark xii.36, Isa. lxiii.10,11, Luke i.15.) What the expression does mean is this: The Holy Ghost was not yet with men in such fullness of influence on their minds, hearts, and understandings, as the Spirit of adoption and revelation, as He was after our Lord ascended up into heaven. It is clear as daylight, from our Lord's language about the Spirit in John xiv.16,17,26, xv.26, and xvi.7-15, that believers were meant to receive a far more full and complete outpouring of the Holy Spirit after His ascension than they had received before. It is a simple matter of fact, indeed, that after the ascension the Apostles were quite different men from what they had been before. They both saw, spoke, and acted like men grown up, while before the ascension they had been like children. It was this increased light and knowledge and decision that made them such a blessing to the world, far more than any miraculous gifts. The possession of the gifts of the Spirit, it is evident, in the early Church was quite compatible with an ungodly heart. A man might speak with tongues and yet be like salt that had lost its savor. The possession of the fullness of the graces of the Spirit, on the contrary, was that which made any man a blessing to the world.Alford says: "St. John does not say that the words were a prophecy of what happened on the day of Pentecost, but of the Spirit which the believers were about to receive. Their first reception of Him must not be illogically put in the place of all His indwelling and working, which are here intended."I am quite aware that most commentators hold that the outpouring of the Spirit at Pentecost was specially meant by St. John in this passage. But after carefully considering the matter, I cannot subscribe to this opinion. To confine this verse to the day of Pentecost appears to me to cramp and narrow its meaning—to deprive many believers of their interest in a most precious promise and to overlook all the special language about the inward teaching of the Comforter as a thing to come on believers, which our Lord used the night before His crucifixion.Bengel remarks that the use of "to be" instead of "to be present" is not uncommon in the Bible. Thus (2 Chron. xv.3.) When therefore we read "the Holy Ghost was not," we need not be stumbled by the expression. It simply means "He was not fully manifested and poured out on the Church." Peter, James, and John no doubt had the Spirit now, when our Lord was speaking. But they had Him much more fully after our Lord was glorified. This explains the meaning of the passage before us. We should note, in leaving these three verses, what a striking example they supply to preachers, ministers, and teachers of religion. Let such learn from their

Master to offer Christ boldly, freely, fully, broadly, unconditionally to all thirsting souls. The Gospel is too often spoiled in the presentation of it. Some fence it round with conditions and keep sinners at a distance. Others direct sinners wrongly and send them to something else beside or instead of Christ. He only copies his Lord who says, "If anyone feels his sins, let him come at once, straight, direct; not merely to church, or to the sacrament, or to repentance, or to prayer, but to Christ Himself."

Chapter Eight

Inspiration

"All Scripture is given by inspiration of God." [2 Tim 3:16]

How was the Bible written?-"Whence is it? From heaven, or of men?"-Had the writers of the Bible any special or peculiar help in doing their work?-Is there anything in the Bible which makes it unlike all other books, and therefore demands our respectful attention? These are questions of vast importance. They are questions to which I wish to offer an answer in this paper. To speak plainly, the subject I propose to examine is that deep one, the inspiration of Scripture. I believe the Bible to have been written by inspiration of God, and I want others to be of the same belief.

The subject is always important. I place it purposely in the very forefront of the papers which compose this volume. I ask a hearing for the doctrines which I am about to handle, because they are drawn from a book which is the "Word of God." Inspiration, in short, is the very keel and foundation of Christianity. If Christians have no Divine book to turn to as the warrant of their doctrine and practice, they have no solid ground for present peace or hope, and no right to claim the attention of mankind. They are building on a quicksand, and their faith is vain. We ought to be able to say boldly, "We are what we are, and we do what we do, because we have here a book which we believe to be the "Word of God."

The subject is one of peculiar importance in the present day. Infidelity and skepticism abound everywhere. In one form or another they are to be found in every rank and class of society. Thousands of Englishmen are not ashamed to say that they regard the Bible as an old obsolete Jewish book, which has no special claim on our faith and obedience, and that it contains many inaccuracies and defects. Myriads who will not go so far as this are wavering and shaken in their belief, and show plainly by their lives that they are not quite sure the Bible is true. In a day like this the true Christian should be able to set his foot down firmly, and to render a reason of his confidence in God's Word. He should be able by sound arguments to meet and silence the gainsayer, if he cannot convince him. He should be able to show good cause why he thinks the Bible is "from heaven, and not of men."

The subject without doubt is a very difficult one. It cannot be followed up without entering on ground which is dark and mysterious to mortal man. It involves the discussion of things which are miraculous, and supernatural, and above reason, and cannot be fully explained. But difficulties must not turn us away from any subject in religion. There is not a science in the world about which questions may not be asked which no one can answer. It is poor philosophy to say we will believe nothing unless we can understand everything! We must not give up the subject of inspiration in despair because it contains things "hard to be understood." There still remains a vast amount of ground which is plain to every common understanding. I invite my readers to occupy this ground with me today, and to hear what I have got to say on the Divine authority of God's Word.

In considering the subject before us, there are two things which I propose to do:-

I. In the first place, I shall try to show the general truth, *that the Bible is given by inspiration of God.*

II. In the second place, I shall try to show *the extent to which the Bible is inspired.*

I trust that all who read this paper will take up the subject in a serious and reverent spirit. This question of inspiration is no light one. It involves tremendously grave consequences. If the Bible is not the Word of God and inspired, the whole of Christendom for 1800 years has been under an immense delusion; half the human race has been cheated and deceived, and churches are monuments of folly.-If the Bible is the Word of God and inspired, all who refuse to believe it are in fearful danger;-they are living on the brink of eternal misery. No man, in his sober senses, can fail to see that the whole subject demands most serious attention.

I. In the first place, I propose to show the general truth,-*that the Bible is given by inspiration of God.*

In saying this, I mean to assert that the Bible is utterly unlike all other books that were ever written, because its writers were specially inspired, or enabled by God, for the work which they did. I say that the Book comes to us with a claim which no other book possesses. It is stamped with Divine authority. In this respect it stands entirely alone. Sermons, and tracts, and theological writings of all kinds, may be sound and edifying, but they are only the handiwork of uninspired man. The Bible alone is the Book of God.

Now I shall not waste time in proving that the Scriptures are genuine and authentic, that they were really written by the very men who profess to have written them, and that they contain the very things which they wrote. I shall not touch what are commonly called external evidences. I shall bring forward the book itself, and put it in the witness box. I shall try to show that nothing can possibly account for the Bible being what it is, and doing what it has done, except the theory that it is the Word of God. I lay it down broadly, as a position which cannot be turned, that the Bible itself, fairly examined, is the best witness of its own inspiration. I shall content myself with stating some plain facts about the Bible, which can neither be denied nor explained away. And the ground I shall take up is this,-that these facts ought to satisfy every reasonable inquirer that the Bible is of God, and not of man. They are simple facts, which require no knowledge of Hebrew, or Greek, or Latin, in order to be understood; yet they are facts which prove to my own mind conclusively that the Bible is superhuman, or not of man.

(a) It is a fact, that there is *an extraordinary fullness and richness in the contents of the Bible.* It throws more light on a vast number of most important subjects than all the other books in the world put together. It boldly handles matters which are beyond the reach of man, when left to himself. It treats of things which are mysterious and invisible,-the soul, the world to come, and eternity, depths which man has no line to fathom. All who have tried to write of these things, without Bible light, have done little but show their own ignorance. They grope like the blind; they speculate; they guess; they generally make the darkness more visible, and land us in a region of uncertainty and doubt. How dim were the views of Socrates, Plato, Cicero, and Seneca! A well-taught Sunday scholar, in this day, knows more spiritual truth than all these sages put together.

The Bible alone gives a reasonable account of the *beginning and end of the globe* on which we live. It starts from the birthday of sun, moon, stars, and earth in their present order, and shows us creation in its cradle. It foretells the dissolution of all things, when the earth and all its works shall be burned up, and shows us creation in its grave. It tells us the story of the world's youth; and it tells us the story of its old age. It gives us a picture of its first days; and it gives us a picture of its last. How vast and important is this knowledge! Can this be the handiwork of uninspired man? Let us try to answer that question.

The Bible alone gives a *true and faithful account of man*. It does not flatter him as novels and romances do; it does not conceal his faults and exaggerate his goodness; it paints him just as he is. It describes him as a fallen creature, of his own nature inclined to evil,-a creature needing not only a pardon, but a new heart, to make him fit for heaven. It shows him to be a corrupt being under every circumstance, when left to himself,-corrupt after the loss of paradise,-corrupt after the flood,-corrupt when fenced in by divine laws and commandments, corrupt when the Son of God came down and visited him in the flesh,-corrupt in the face of warnings, promises, miracles, judgments, mercies. In one word, it shows man to be by nature always a sinner. How important is this knowledge! Can this be the work of uninspired minds? Let us try to answer that question.

The Bible alone gives us *true views of God*. By nature man knows nothing clearly or fully about Him. All his conceptions of Him are low, groveling, and debased. What could be more degraded than the gods of the Canaanites and Egyptians,-of Babylon, of Greece, and of Rome? What can be more vile than the gods of the Hindus and other heathen in our own time?-By the Bible we know that *God hates sin*. The destruction of the old world by the flood; the burning of Sodom and Gomorrah; the drowning of Pharaoh and the Egyptians in the Red Sea; the cutting off the nations of Canaan; the overthrow of Jerusalem and the Temple; the scattering of the Jews; all these are unmistakable witnesses.-By the Bible we know that *God loves sinners*. His gracious promise in the day of Adam's fall; His longsuffering in the time of Noah; His deliverance of Israel out of the land of Egypt; His gift of the law at Mount Sinai; His bringing the tribes into the promised land; His forbearance in the days of the Judges and Kings; His repeated warnings by the mouth of His prophets; His restoration of Israel after the Babylonian captivity; His sending His Son into the world, in due time, to be crucified; His commanding the Gospel to be preached to the Gentiles, all these are speaking facts.-By the Bible we learn that *God knows all things*. We see Him foretelling things hundreds and thousands of years before they take place, and as He foretells so it comes to pass. He foretold that the family of Ham should be a servant of servants,-that Tyre should become a rock for drying nets,-that Nineveh should become a desolation,-that Babylon should be made a desert-that Egypt should be the basest of kingdoms, that Edom should be forsaken and uninhabited,-and that the Jews should not be reckoned among the nations. All these things were utterly unlikely and improbable. Yet all have been fulfilled. Once more I say, how vast and important all this knowledge is! Can this Book be the work of uninspired man? Let us try to answer that question.

The Bible alone teaches us that *God has made a full, per feet, and complete provision for the salvation of fallen man*. It tells of an atonement made for the sin of the world, by the sacrifice and death of God's own Son upon the cross. It tells us that by His death for sinners, as their Substitute, He obtained eternal redemption for all that believe on Him. The claims of God's broken law have now been satisfied. Christ has suffered for sin, the just for the unjust. God can now be just and yet the justifier of the ungodly. It tells us that there is now a complete remedy for the guilt of sin,-even the precious blood of Christ; and peace, and rest of conscience for all who believe on Christ. "Whosoever believeth on Him shall not perish, but have eternal life." It tells us that there is a complete remedy for the power of sin,-even the almighty grace of the Spirit of Christ. It shows us the Holy Ghost quickening believers, and making them new creatures. It promises a new heart and a new nature to all who will hear Christ's voice, and follow Him. Once more I say, how important this knowledge is! What should we know of all this comfortable truth without the Bible? Can this Book be the composition of uninspired men? Let us try to answer that question.

The Bible alone *explains the state of things that we see in the world around us.* There are many things on earth which a natural man cannot explain. The amazing inequality of conditions,-the poverty and distress; the oppression and persecution,-the shakings and tumults,-the failures of statesmen and legislators,-the constant existence of uncured evils and abuses,-all these things are often puzzling to him. He sees, but does not understand. But the Bible makes it all clear. The Bible can tell him that the whole world lieth in wickedness; that the prince of the world, the devil, is everywhere,-and that it is vain to look for perfection in the present order of things. The Bible will tell him that neither laws nor education can ever change men's hearts,-and that just as no man will ever make a machine work well, unless he allows for friction,-so also no man will do much good in the world, unless he always remembers that human nature is fallen, and that the world he works in is full of sin. The Bible will tell him that there is "a good time" certainly coming,-and coming per-haps sooner than people expect it,-a time of perfect knowledge, perfect justice, perfect happiness, and perfect peace. But the Bible will tell him this time shall not be brought in by any power but that of Christ coming to earth again. And for that second coming of Christ, the Bible will tell him to prepare. Once more, I say, how important is all this knowledge!

All these are things which men could find nowhere except in the Scriptures. We have probably not the least idea how little we should know about these things if we had not the Bible. We hardly know the value of the air we breathe, and the sun which shines on us, because we have never known what it is to be without them. We do not value the truths on which I have been just now dwelling, because we do not realize the darkness of men to whom these truths have not been revealed. Surely no tongue can fully tell the value of the treasures this one volume contains. Set down that fact in your mind, and do not forget it. The extraordinary contents of the Bible are a great fact which can only be explained by admitting its inspiration. Mark well what I say. It is a simple broad fact that, in the matter of contents, the Bible stands entirely alone, and no other book is fit to be named in the same day with it. He that dares to say the Bible is not inspired, let him give a reasonable account of this fact, if he can.

(b) It is another fact that there is an *extraordinary unity and harmony in the contents of the Bible,* which is entirely above man. We all know how difficult it is to get a story told by any three persons, not living together, in which there are not some contradictions and discrepancies. If the story is a long one, and involves a large quantity of particulars, unity seems almost impossible among the common run of men. But it is not so with the Bible. Here is a long book written by not less than thirty different persons. The writers were men of every rank and class in society. One was a lawgiver. One was a warlike king. One was a peaceful king. One was a herdsman. One had been brought up as a publican, another as a physician, another as a learned Pharisee, two as fishermen,-several as priests. They lived at different intervals over a space of 1500 years; and the greater part of them never saw each other face to face. And yet there is a perfect harmony among all these writers? They all write as if they were under one dictation. The style and hand-writing may vary, but the mind that runs through their work is always one and the same. They all tell the same story. They all give one account of man,-one account of God,-one account of the way of salvation,-one account of the human heart. You see truth unfolding under their hands as you go through the volume of their writings,-but you never detect any real contradiction, or contrariety of view.

Let us set down this fact in our minds, and ponder it well. Tell us not that this unity might be the result of chance. No one can ever believe that but a very credulous person. There is only one satisfactory account to be given of the fact before us.-The Bible is not of man, but of God.

(c) It is another fact that there is *an extraordinary wisdom, sublimity and majesty in the style of the Bible,* which is above man. Strange and unlikely as it was, the writers of Scripture have produced a book which even at this day is utterly unrivalled. With all our boasted attainments in science and art and learning, we can produce nothing that can be compared with the Bible. Even at this very hour, in 1877, the book stands entirely alone. There is a strain and a style and a tone of thought about it, which separate it from all other writings. There are no weak points, and motes, and flaws, and blemishes. There is no mixture of infirmity and feebleness, such as you will find in the works of even the best Christians. "Holy, holy, holy," seems written on every page. To talk of comparing the Bible with other "sacred books" so called, such as the Koran, the Shasters, or the book of Mormon, is positively absurd. You might as well compare the sun with a rushlight,-or Skiddaw with a molehill,-or St. Paul's with an Irish hovel,-or the Portland vase with a garden pot,-or the Kohinoor diamond with a bit of glass.1 God seems to have allowed the existence of these pretended revelations, in order to prove the immeasurable superiority of His own Word. To talk of the inspiration of the Bible, as only differing in degree from that of such writings as the works of Homer, Plato, Shakespeare, Dante, and Milton, is simply a piece of blasphemous folly. Every honest and unprejudiced reader must see that there is a gulf between the Bible and any other book, which no man can fathom. You feel, on turning from the Scriptures to other works, that you have got into a new atmosphere. You feel like one who has exchanged gold for base metal, and heaven for earth. And how can this mighty difference be accounted for? The men who wrote the Bible had no special advantages. They lived in a remote corner of the civilized earth. They had, most of them, little leisure, few books, and no learning,-such as learning is reckoned in this world. Yet the book they compose is one which is unrivalled! There is but one way of accounting for this fact. *They wrote under the direct inspiration of God.*

(d) It is another fact that there is *an extraordinary accuracy in the facts and statements of the Bible, which is above man.* Here is a book which has been finished and before the world for nearly 1800 years. These 1800 years have been the busiest and most changeful period the world has ever seen. During this period the greatest discoveries have been made in science, the greatest alterations in the ways and customs of society, the greatest improvements in the habits and usages of life. Hundreds of things might be named which satisfied and pleased our forefathers, which we have laid aside long ago as obsolete, useless, and old-fashioned. The laws, the books, the houses, the furniture, the clothes, the arms, the machinery, the carriages of each succeeding century, have been a continual improvement on those of the century that went before. There is hardly a thing in which faults and weak points have not been discovered. There is scarcely an institution which has not gone through a process of sifting, purifying, refining, simplifying, reforming, amending, and changing. But all this time men have never discovered a weak point or a defect in the Bible. Infidels have assailed it in vain. There it stands,-perfect, and fresh, and complete, as it did eighteen centuries ago. The march of intellect never overtakes it. The wisdom of wise men never gets beyond it. The science of philosophers never proves it wrong. The discoveries of travellers never convict it of mistakes.-Are the distant islands of the Pacific laid open? Nothing is found that in the slightest degree contradicts the Bible account of man's heart.-Are the ruins of Nineveh and Egypt ransacked and explored? Nothing is found that overturns one jot or tittle of the Bible's historical statements.-How shall we account for this fact? Who could have thought it possible that so large a book, handling such a vast variety of subjects, should at the end of 1800 years, be found so free from erroneous statements? There is only one account to be given of the fact.-*The Bible was written by inspiration of God.*

(e) It is another fact that there is in the Bible *an extraordinary suitableness to the spiritual wants of all mankind.* It exactly meets the heart of man in every rank or class, in every country and climate, in every age and period of life. It is the only book in existence which is never out of place and out of date. Other books after a time become obsolete and old-fashioned: the Bible never does. Other books suit one country or people, and not another: the Bible suits all. It is the book of the poor and unlearned no less than of the rich and the philosopher. It feeds the mind of the labourer in his cottage, and it satisfies the gigantic intellects of Newton, Chalmers, Brewster, and Faraday. Lord Macaulay, and John Bright, and the writers of brilliant articles in the Times, are all under obligations to the same volume. It is equally valued by the converted New

Zealander in the southern hemisphere, and the Red River Indian in the cold north of America, and the Hindu under the tropical sun.

It is the only book, moreover, which seems always fresh and evergreen and new. For eighteen centuries it has been studied and prayed over by millions of private Christians, and expounded and explained and preached to us by thousands of ministers. Fathers, and Schoolmen, and Reformers, and Puritans, and modern divines, have incessantly dug down into the mine of Scripture, and yet have never exhausted it. It is a well never dry, and a field which is never barren. It meets the hearts and minds and consciences of Christians in the nineteenth century as fully as it did those of Greeks and Romans when it was first completed. It suits the "Dairyman's daughter" as well as Persis, or Tryphena, or Tryphosa,-and the English Peer as well as the converted African at Sierra Leone. It is still the first book which fits the child's mind when he begins to learn religion, and the last to which the old man clings as he leaves the world.2 In short, it suits all ages, ranks, climates, minds, conditions. It is the one book which suits the world.

Now how shall we account for this singular fact? What satisfactory explanation can we give? There is only one account and explanation.-*T he Bible was written by Divine inspiration.* It is the book of the world, because He inspired it who formed the world,-who made all nations of one blood,-and knows man's common nature. It is the book for every heart, because He dictated it who alone knows all hearts, and what all hearts require. *It is the book of God.*

(f) Last, but not least, it is a great fact that *the Bible has had a most extraordinary effect on the condition of those nations in which it has been known, taught, and read.*

I invite any honest-minded reader to look at a map of the world, and see what a story that map tells. Which are the countries on the face of the globe at this moment where there is the greatest amount of idolatry, or cruelty, or tyranny, or impurity, or misgovernment, or disregard of life and liberty and truth? Precisely those countries where the Bible is not known.-Which are the Christian countries, so-called, where the greatest quantity of ignorance, superstition, and corruption, is to be found at this very moment? The countries in which the Bible is a forbidden or neglected book, such countries as Spain and the South American State s.-Which are the countries where liberty, and public and private morality have attained the highest pitch? The countries where the Bible is free to all, like England, Scotland, Germany, and the United States. Yes! when you know how a nation deals with the Bible, you may generally know what a nation is.

But this is not all. Let us look nearer home. Which are the cities on earth where the fewest soldiers and police are required to keep order? London, Manchester, Liverpool, New York, Philadelphia,-cities where Bibles abound. -Which are the countries in Europe where there are the fewest murders and illegitimate births? The Protestant countries, where the Bible is freely read.-Which are the Churches and religious bodies on earth which are producing the greatest results by spreading light and dispelling darkness? Those which make much of the Bible, and teach and preach it as God's Word. The Romanist, the Neologian, the Socinian, the deist, the sceptic, or the friends of mere secular teaching, have never yet shown us one Sierra Leone, one New Zealand, one Tinnevelly, as the fruit of their principles. We only can do that who honour the Bible and reverence it as God's Word. Let this fact also be remembered. He that denies the Divine inspiration of the Bible, let him explain this fact if he can.3

I place these six facts about the Bible before my readers, and I ask them to consider them well. Take them all six together, treat them fairly, and look at them honestly. Upon any other principle than that of divine inspiration, those six facts appear to me inexplicable and unaccountable. Here is a book written by a succession of Jews, in a little corner of the world, which positively stands alone. Not only were its writers isolated and cut off in a peculiar manner from other nations, but they belonged to a people who have never produced any other hook of note except the Bible! There is not the slightest proof that, unassisted and left to themselves, they were capable of writing anything remarkable, like the Greeks and Romans. Yet these men have given the world a volume which for depth, unity, sublimity, accuracy, suitableness to the wants of man, and power of influencing its readers, is perfectly unrivalled. How can this be explained? How can it be accounted for? To my mind there is only one answer. The writers of the Bible were divinely helped and qualified for the work which they did. The book which they have given to us was written by inspiration of God.4

For my own part, I believe that in dealing with sceptics, and unbelievers, and enemies of the Bible, Christians are too apt to stand only on the defensive. They are too often content with answering this or that little objection, or discussing this or that little difficulty, which is picked out of Scripture and thrown in their teeth. I believe we ought to act on the aggressive far more than we do, and to press home on the adversaries of inspiration the enormous difficulties of their own position. We have a right to ask them, how can they possibly explain the origin and nature of the Bible, if they will not allow that it is of Divine authority? We have a right to say,-"Here is a book which not only courts inquiry but demands investigation. We challenge you to tell us how that Book was written."-How can they account for this Book standing so entirely alone, and for nothing having ever been written equal to it, like it, near it, or fit to be compared with it for a minute? I defy them to give any rational reply on their own principles. On our principles we can. To tell us that man's unassisted mind could have written the Bible is simply ridiculous. It is worse than ridiculous it is the height of credulity. In short, the difficulties of unbelief are far greater than the difficulties of faith. No doubt there are things "hard to be understood" if we accept the Scriptures as God's Word. But, after all, they are nothing compared to the hard things which rise up in our way, and demand solution if we once deny inspiration. There is no alternative. Men must either believe things which are grossly improbable, or else they must accept the great general truth that *the Bible is the inspired Word of God.*

II. The second thing which I propose to consider is *the extent to which the Bible is inspired.* Assuming, as a general truth, that the Bible is given by Divine inspiration, I wish to examine how far and to what degree its writers received Divine help. In short, what is it exactly that we mean when we talk of the Scriptures as "the Word of God"?

This is, no doubt, a difficult question, and one about which the best Christians are not entirely of one mind. The plain truth is that inspiration is a *miracle*; and, like all miracles, there is much about it which we cannot fully understand.-We must not confound it with intellectual power, such as great poets and authors possess. To talk of Shakespeare and Milton and Byron being inspired, like Moses and St. Paul, is to my mind almost profane.-Nor must we confound it with the gifts and graces bestowed on the early Christians in the primitive Church. All the Apostles were enabled to preach and work miracles, but not all were inspired to write.-We must rather regard it as a special supernatural gift, bestowed on about thirty people out of mankind, in order to qualify them for the special business of writing the Scriptures; and we must be content to allow that, like everything miraculous, we cannot entirely explain it, though we can believe it. A miracle would not be a miracle, if it could be explained. That miracles are possible, I do not stop to prove here. I never trouble myself on that subject until those who deny miracles have fairly grappled with the great fact that Christ rose again from the dead. I firmly believe that miracles are possible, and have been wrought; and among great miracles I place the fact that men were inspired by God to write the Bible. Inspiration, therefore, being a miracle, I frankly allow that there are difficulties about it which at present I cannot fully solve.

The exact manner in which the minds of the inspired writers of Scripture worked when they wrote, I do not pretend to explain. Very likely they could not have explained it themselves. I do not admit for a moment that they were mere machines holding pens, and, like type-setters in a printing-office, did not understand what they were doing. I abhor the "mechanical" theory of inspiration. I dislike the idea that men like Moses and St. Paul were no better than organ pipes, employed by the Holy Ghost, or ignorant secretaries or amanuenses who wrote by dictation what they did not understand. I admit nothing of the kind. I believe that in some marvelous manner the Holy Ghost made use of the reason, the memory, the intellect, the style of thought, and the peculiar mental temperament of each writer of the Scriptures. But how and in what manner this was done I can no more explain than I can the union of two natures, God and man, in the person of our blessed Lord Jesus Christ. I only know that there is both a Divine and a human element in the Bible, and that while the men who wrote it were really and truly men, the book that they wrote and handed down to us is really and truly the Word of God. I know the result, but I do not understand the process. The result is, that the Bible is the written Word of God; but I can no more explain the process than I can explain how the water became wine at Cana, or how five loaves fed five thousand men, or how a word raised Lazarus from the dead. I do not pretend to explain miracles, and I do not pretend to explain fully the miraculous gift of inspiration. The position I take up is that, while the Bible-writers were not "machines," as some sneeringly say, they only wrote what God taught them to write. The Holy Ghost put into their minds thoughts and ideas, and then guided their pens in writing them. When you read the Bible you are not reading the unaided, self-taught composition of erring men like ourselves, but thoughts and words which were suggested by the eternal God. The men who were employed to indite the Scripture spake not of themselves. They "spake as they were moved by the Holy Ghost." (2 Peter i. 21.) He that holds a Bible in his hand should know that he holds "not the word of man but of God." (1 Thess. ii. 13.) Concerning the precise extent to which the Bible is inspired, I freely admit that Christians differ widely. Some of the views put forth on the subject appear to me erroneous in the extreme. I shall not shrink from giving my own opinion and stating my reasons for maintaining it. In matters like these I dare not call any man master. Painful as it is to disagree with able and gifted men on religious questions, I dare not take up views of inspiration which my head and heart tell me are unsound, however high and honoured the names of those who maintain them. I believe in my conscience that low and defective views of the subject are doing immense damage to the cause of Christ in these last days.

Some hold that some of the books of Scripture are not inspired at all, and have no more authority or claim to our reverence than the writings of any ordinary man. Others who do not go so far as this, and allow that all the books in the Bible are inspired, maintain that inspiration was only partial, and that there are portions in almost every book which are uninspired.-Others hold that inspiration means nothing more than general superintendence and direction, and that, while the Bible writers were miraculously preserved from making mistakes in great things and matters necessary to salvation, in things indifferent they were left to their own unassisted faculties, like any other writers.-Some hold that all the ideas in the Bible were given by inspiration, but not the words and language in which they are clothed,-though how to separate ideas from words it is rather hard to understand!-Some, finally, allow the thorough inspiration of all the Bible, and yet maintain that it was possible for the writers to make occasional mistakes in their statements, and that such mistakes do exist at this day.

From all these views I totally and entirely dissent. They all appear to me more or less defective, below the truth, dangerous in their tendency, and open to grave and insuperable objections. The view which I maintain is that every book, and chapter, and verse, and syllable of the Bible was originally given by inspiration of God. I hold that not only the substance of the Bible, but its language,-not only the ideas of the Bible, but its words; not only certain parts of the Bible, but every chapter of the book,-that all and each are of Divine authority. I hold that the Scripture not only *contains* the Word of God, but *is* the Word of God. I believe the narratives and statements of Genesis, and the catalogues in Chronicles, were just as truly written by inspiration as the Acts of the Apostles. I believe Ezra's account of the nine-and-twenty knives, and St. Paul's message about the cloak and parchments, were as much written under Divine direction as the 20th of Exodus, the 17th of John, or the 8th of Romans. I do not say, be it remembered, that all these parts of the Bible are of equal importance to our souls. Nothing of the kind! But I do say they were all equally given by inspiration.5

In making this statement I ask the reader not to misunderstand my meaning. I do not forget that the Old Testament was written in Hebrew and the New Testament in Greek. The inspiration of every word, for which I contend, is the inspiration of every original Hebrew and Greek word, as the Bible writers first wrote it down. I stand up for nothing more and nothing less than this. I lay no claim to the inspiration of every word in the various versions and translations of God's Word. So far as those translations and versions are faithfully and correctly done, so far they are of equal authority with the original Hebrew and Greek. We have reason to thank God that many of the translations are, in the main, faithful and accurate. At any rate our own English Bible, if not perfect, is so far correct, that in reading it we have a right to believe that we are reading in our own tongue not the word of man; but of God.

Now the view for which I contend,-that every word of the Bible is inspired,-is not accepted by many good Christians, and is bitterly opposed in many quarters. I shall therefore mention a few reasons why it appears to me the only safe and tenable view which can be adopted, and the only one which is free from innumerable objections. If I err in maintaining it I have the comfort, at any rate, of erring in good company. I only take up the same ground which almost all the Fathers occupied; which Bishop Jewell, and Hooker, and Owen, took up long ago; and which Chalmers, Robert Haldane, Gaussen, Bishop Wordsworth, M'Caul, Burgon, and Archdeacon Lee of the Irish Church, have ably defended in modern days. I know, however, that men's minds are variously constituted. Arguments and reasons which appear weighty to some are of no weight with others. I shall content myself with setting down in order the reasons which satisfy me.

(a) For one thing, I cannot see *how the Bible can be a perfect rule of faith and practice* if it is not fully inspired, and if it contains any flaws and imperfections. If the Bible is anything at all it is the statute-book of God's kingdom, the code of laws and regulations by which the subjects of that kingdom are to live,-the register-deed of the terms on which they have peace now and shall have glory hereafter. Now, why are we to suppose that such a book will be loosely and imperfectly drawn up, any more than legal deeds are drawn up on earth? Every lawyer can tell us that in legal deeds and statutes every word is of importance, and that property, life, or death may often turn on a single word. Think of the confusion that would ensue if wills, and settlements, and conveyances, and partnership-deeds, and leases, and agreements, and acts of parliament were not carefully drawn up and carefully interpreted, and every word allowed its due weight. Where would be the use of such documents if particular words went for nothing, and every one had a right to add, or take away, or alter, or deny the validity of words, or erase words at his own discretion? At this rate we might as well lay aside our legal documents altogether. Surely we have a right to expect that in the book which contains our title-deeds for eternity every word will be inspired, and nothing imperfect admitted. If God's statute-book is not inspired, and every word is not of Divine authority, God's subjects are left in a pitiable state. I see much in this.

(b) For another thing, if the Bible is not fully inspired and contains imperfections, I cannot understand the language which is frequently used about it in its own pages. Such expressions as "The oracles of God;"-"He saith;"-"God saith"-"the Holy Ghost spake by Esaias the prophet;" "the Holy Ghost saith, "Today if ye will hear His voice,"-would appear to me inexplicable and extravagant if applied to a book containing occasional blemishes, defects, and mistakes. (Acts vii. 38; Rom. iii. 2; Heb. v. 12; 1 Peter iv. 11; Ephes. iv. 8; Heb. i. 8; Acts xxviii. 25; Heb. iii. 7; x. 15; Rom. ix. 25.) Once grant that every word of Scripture is inspired, and I see an admirable propriety in the language. I cannot understand "the Holy Ghost" making a mistake, or an "oracle" containing anything defective! If any man replies that the Holy Ghost did not *always* speak by Isaiah, I will ask him who is to decide when He did and when He did not? I see much in this.

(c) For another thing, the theory that the Bible was not given by inspiration of God, appears to me utterly *at variance with several quotations from the Old Testament* which I find in the New. I allude to those quotations in which the whole force of the passage turns on one single word, and once even on the use of the singular instead of the plural number. Take, for instance, such quotations as "The Lord said unto my Lord." (Matt. xxii. 44). "I said, Ye are gods." (John x. 34.) "To Abraham and his seed were the promises made. He saith not, And to seeds, as of many; but as of one, And to thy seed, which is Christ." (Gal. iii. 16.)-"He is not ashamed to call them brethren, saying, I will declare Thy name unto my brethren." (Heb. ii. 11, 12.)-In every one these cases the whole point of the quotation lies in a single word.6 But if this is so, it is hard to see on what principle we can deny the inspiration of all the words of Scripture. At any rate, those who deny verbal inspiration will find it difficult to show us which words are inspired and which are not. Who is to draw the line, and where is it to be drawn? I see much in this.

(d) For another thing, *if the words of Scripture are not all inspired, the value of the Bible as a weapon in controversy is greatly damaged*, if not entirely taken away. Who does not know that in arguing with Jews, Arians, or Socinians, the whole point of the texts we quote against them often lies in a single word? What are we to reply if an adversary asserts that the special word of some text, on which we ground an argument, is a mistake of the writer, and therefore of no authority? To my mind it appears that the objection would be fatal. It is useless to quote texts if we once admit that not all the words of which they are composed were given by inspiration. Unless there is some certain standard to appeal to we may as well hold our tongues. Argument is labour in vain if our mouths are to be stopped by the retort, "That text is not inspired." I see much in this.

(e) For another thing, *to give up verbal inspiration appears to me to destroy the usefulness of the Bible as an instrument of public preaching and instruction.* Where is the use of choosing a text and making it the subject of a pulpit address, if we do not believe that every word of the text is inspired? Once let our hearers get hold of the idea that the writers of the Bible could make mistakes in the particular words they used, and they will care little for any reproofs, or exhortations, or remarks which are based on words.-"How do you know," they might ask us, "that this word, about which you made such ado yesterday, was given by the Holy Ghost? How do you know that St. Paul, or St. Peter, or St. John did not make a mistake, and use the wrong word? That they could make mistakes about words you yourself allow."-I know not what others may think. For myself, I could give no answer. I see much in this.

(f) Last, but not least, the denial of verbal inspiration appears to me to *destroy a great part of the usefulness of the Bible as a source of comfort and instruction in private reading.* Where is the true Christian student of the Bible who does not know that words, particular words, afford a large portion of the benefit which he derives from his daily reading? How much the value of many a cherished text depends on some single phrase, or the number of a substantive, or the tense of a verb? Alas! there would be an end of all this if we once concede that each word is not inspired; and that, for anything we know, some much loved favourite substantive, or verb, or pronoun, or adverb, or adjective, was an Apostle's mistake, and the word of man, not of God! What others might think I know not. For myself, I should be tempted to lay aside my Bible in despair, and become of all men most miserable. I see much in this.

Now, I freely grant that many excellent Christians think that the view I maintain is open to serious objections. That the Bible, generally speaking, is given by inspiration, they firmly maintain. But they shrink from maintaining that inspiration extends to every word of Scripture. I am sorry to differ from these worthy people. But I cannot see the weight and force of their objections. Fairly and honestly examined, they fail to carry conviction to my mind.

(a) Some object that there are occasional statements in the Bible which *contradict the facts of history.* Are these all verbally inspired?-My answer is that it is far more easy to assert this than to prove it. There is nothing of which we have so few trustworthy remains as very ancient history, and if ancient uninspired history and Bible history seem to disagree, it is generally safer and wiser to believe that Bible history is right and other history wrong. At any rate, it is a singular fact that all recent researches in Assyria, Babylon, Palestine, and Egypt, show an extraordinary tendency to confirm the perfect accuracy of the Word of God. The lamented Mr. Smith's discoveries at Babylon are a remarkable example of what I mean. There are buried evidences which God seems to keep in reserve for these last days. If Bible history and other histories cannot be made to agree at present, it is safest to wait.

(b) Some object that there are occasional statements in the Bible which *contradict the facts of natural science.* Are these all inspired?-My answer is again, that it is far more easy to assert this than to prove it. The Bible was not written to teach a system of geology, botany, or astronomy, or a history of birds, insects, and animals, and on matters touching these subjects it wisely uses popular language, such as common people can understand. No one thinks of saying that the Astronomer Royal contradicts science because he speaks of the sun's "rising and setting." If the Bible said anywhere that the earth was a flat surface,-or that it was a fixed globe round which the sun revolved,-or that it never existed in any state before Adam and Eve,-there might be something in the objection. But it never does so. It speaks of scientific subjects as they appear. But it never flatly contradicts science.7

(c) Some object that there are occasional statements in the Bible which are *monstrous, absurd, and incredible.* Are they really obliged to believe that Eve was tempted by the devil in the form of a serpent,-that Noah was saved in an ark,-that the Israelites crossed the Red Sea between two walls of water,-that Balaam's ass spoke, and that Jonah actually went into the whale's belly? Are all these statements inspired?-My answer is that Christ's apostles speak of these things as historical facts, and were more likely to know the truth about them than we are. After all, do we believe in miracles or not? Do we believe that Christ Himself rose from the dead? Let us stick to that one grand miracle first, and disprove it if we can. If we do believe it, it is foolish to object to things because they are miraculous.

(d) Some object that there are things mentioned occasionally in the Bible which are so *trifling* that they are unworthy to be called inspired. They point to St. Paul's writing about his cloak, and books, and parchments, and ask if we really think that the Apostle wrote about such little matters by inspiration of God?-I answer that the least things affecting any of God's children are not too small for the notice of Him who "numbers the hairs of our heads." There are excellent and edifying lessons to be learned from the cloak and the parchments, as Robert Haldane has shown most convincingly, in his work on the Evidences of Divine Revelation. After all, man knows very little what is great and what is small in God's sight. The history of Nimrod "the mighty hunter" is dispatched in three verses of Genesis, and the history of a Syrian dwelling in tents, called Abraham, fills up no less than fourteen chapters. The microscope applied to the book of nature, can show us God's hand in the least lichen that grows on the top of Scawfell as well as in the cedar of Lebanon. The veriest trifles, as they seem to us in the Book of Scripture, may turn out to be most striking confirmations of its truth. Paley has shown this admirably in his "Horae Paulinae," and Professor Blunt in his "Undesigned Coincidences."

(e) Some object that there are grave discrepancies in some of the *Bible histories,* especially in the four Gospels, which *cannot be made to harmonize and agree.* Are the words, they ask, all inspired in these cases? Have the writers made no mistakes?-I answer that the number of these discrepancies is grossly exaggerated, and that in many cases they are only apparent, and disappear under the touch of common sense. Even in the hardest of them we should remember, in common fairness, that circumstances are very likely kept back from us which entirely reconcile everything, if we only knew them. Very often in these days when two honest, veracious men give a separate account of some long story, their accounts do not quite tally, because one dwells on one part and the other on another. All well-informed students of history know that the precise day when Charles I erected his standard at Nottingham, in the Parliamentary war, has not been settled to this hour.

(f) Some object that *Job's friends,* in their long speeches, *said many weak and foolish things.* Were all their words inspired?-An objection like this arises from an illogical and confused idea of what inspiration means. The book of Job contains an historical account of a wonderful part of the old patriarch's history, and a report both of his speeches and of those of his friends. But we are nowhere told that either Job or Eliphaz and his companions spoke all that they spoke by the Holy Ghost. The writer of the book of Job was thoroughly inspired to record all they said. But whether they spoke rightly or wrongly is to be decided by the general teaching of Scripture. No one would say that St. Peter was inspired when he said, "I know not the Man," in the High Priest's palace. But the writer of the Gospel was inspired when he wrote it down for our learning. In the Acts of the Apostles the letter of Claudius Lysias was certainly not written by inspiration, and Gamaliel, and the town clerk of Ephesus and Tertullus were not inspired when they made their speeches. But it is equally certain that St. Luke was inspired to write them down and record them in his book.

(g) Some object that St. Paul, *in the 7th chapter of the 1st epistle to the Corinthians*, when giving certain advice to the Corinthian Church, says at one time, "Not I, but the Lord," and at another, "I, not the Lord." And they ask, Does not this show that in part of his advice he was not inspired?-I answer, Not at all. A careful study of the chapter will show that when the Apostle says "Not I, but the Lord," he lays down some principles on which the Lord had spoken already; and when he says "I, not the Lord," he gives advice on some point about which there had been no revelation hitherto. But there is not the slightest proof that he is not writing all the way through under direct inspiration of God.

(h) Some object that there are *many various readings* of the words of Scripture, and that we cannot, therefore, feel sure that we have the original inspired Word of God. I answer that the various readings, when fairly examined, will prove to be absurdly exaggerated in number and importance. Dr. Kennicott, Bengel, and others have proved this long ago. No doubt we may have lost a few of the original words. We have no right to expect infallibility in transcribers and copyists, before the invention of printing. But there is not a single doctrine in Scripture which would be affected or altered if all the various readings were allowed, and all the disputed or doubtful words were omitted. Considering how many hands the Bible passed through before printing was invented, and who the transcribers were, it is marvellous that the various readings are so few! The fact that about the immense majority of all the words in the old Hebrew and Greek Scriptures there is no doubt at all, is little short of a miracle, and demands much thanksgiving to God. One thing is very certain. There is no ancient book which has been handed down to us with so good a text and so few various readings as the Bible.

(i) Finally, some object that occasional parts of the Bible are taken out, copied, and *extracted from the writings of uninspired men*, such as historical chronicles, and pedigrees, and lists of names. Are all these to be regarded as inspired?-I reply that there seems no reason why the Holy Ghost should not direct the Bible writers to use materials made ready to their hands, as well as facts which they had seen themselves, and by so directing them, invested such words as they used with Divine authority. When St. Paul quoted lines from heathen poets he did not mean us to regard them as inspired. But he was taught by God to clothe his ideas in the words which they had used, and by so doing he very likely obtained a favourable reading from many. And when we read such quotations, or read lists of names taken from Jewish chronicles and registers, we need not doubt that Bible writers were taught to use such materials by inspiration of God.

I leave the objections to verbal inspiration at this point, and will detain my readers no longer with them. I will not pretend to deny that the subject has its difficulties, which will probably never be completely solved. I cannot perhaps clear up such difficulties as the mention of "Jeremy the prophet" in Matthew xxvii., or reconcile the third and sixth hour in St. John's and St. Mark's account of the crucifixion, or explain Stephen's account of Jacob's burial in the seventh chapter of Acts, to my own entire satisfaction. But I have no doubt *these difficulties can be explained*, and perhaps will be some day. These things do not move me.

I expect difficulties in such a deep and miraculous matter as inspiration, which I have not eyes to see through. I am content to wait. It was a wise saying of Faraday, that "there are many questions about which it is the highest philosophy to keep our minds in a state of judicious suspense." It should be a settled rule with us never to give up a great principle, when we have got hold of it, on account of difficulties. Time often makes things clear which at first look dark. The view of inspiration which presents to my own mind the fewest difficulties, is that in which all the words of Scripture, as well as the thoughts, are regarded as inspired. Here I take my stand.

Remember what I have just said. Never give up a great principle in theology on account of difficulties. Wait patiently, and the difficulties may all melt away. Let that be an axiom in your mind. Suffer me to mention an illustration of what I mean. Persons who are conversant with astronomy know that before the discovery of the planet Neptune there were difficulties which greatly troubled the most scientific astronomers, respecting certain aberrations of the planet Uranus. These aberrations puzzled the minds of astronomers; and some of them suggested that they might possibly prove the whole Newtonian system to be untrue. But just at that time a well-known French astronomer, named Leverrier, read before the Academy of Science at Paris a paper, in which he laid down this great axiom, that it did not become a scientific man to give up a principle because of difficulties which apparently could not be explained. He said in effect, "We cannot explain the aberrations of Uranus now; but we may be sure that the Newtonian system will be proved to be right, sooner or later. Something may be discovered one day which will prove that these aberrations may be accounted for, and yet the Newtonian system remain true and unshaken." A few years after, the anxious eyes of astronomers discovered the last great planet, Neptune. This planet was shown to be the true cause of all the aberrations of Uranus; and what the French astronomer had laid down as a principle in science was proved to be wise and true. The application of the anecdote is obvious. Let us beware of giving up any first principle in theology. Let us not give up the great principle of plenary verbal inspiration because of apparent difficulties. The day may come when they will all be solved. In the meantime we may rest assured that the difficulties which beset any other theory of inspiration are tenfold greater than any which beset our own.

Let me now conclude this paper with a few words of plain application. Let us lay aside all deep discussion of hard things about the manner of inspiration. Let us take it for granted that, in some way or other, whether we can explain it or not, we hold the Bible to be the Word of God. Let us start from this point. Let my readers give me a hearing, while I say a few things which appear to me to deserve their attention.

1. Is the Bible the Word of God? Then mind that you do not neglect it. Read it! read it! Begin to read it this very day. What greater insult to God can a man be guilty of than to refuse to read the letter God sends him from heaven? Oh, be sure, if you will not read your Bible, you are in fearful danger of losing your soul!

You are in danger, because *God will reckon with you for your neglect of the Bible in the day of judgment.* You will have to give account of your use of time, strength, and money; and you will also have to give account of your use of the Word. You will not stand at that bar on the same level, in point of responsibility, with the dweller in central Africa, who never heard of the Bible. Oh, no! To whom much is given, of them much will be required. Of all men's buried talents, none will weigh them down so heavily as a neglected Bible. As you deal with the Bible, so God will deal with your soul. Will you not repent and turn over a new leaf in life, and read your Bible?

You are in danger, because *there is no degree of error in religion into which you may not fall.* You are at the mercy of the first clever Jesuit, Mormonite, Socinian, Turk, or Jew, who may happen to meet you. A land of unwalled villages is not more defenseless against an enemy than a man who neglects his Bible. You may go on tumbling from one step of delusion to another, till at length you are landed in the pit of hell. I say once more, Will you not repent and read your Bible?

You are in danger, because *there is not a single reasonable excuse you can allege for neglecting the Bible.* You have no time to read it forsooth! But you can make time for eating, drinking, sleeping, getting money and spending money, and perhaps for newspaper reading and smoking. You might easily make time to read the Word. Alas, it is not want of time, but waste of time that ruins souls!-You find it too troublesome to read, forsooth! You had better say at once it is too much trouble to go to heaven, and you are content to go to hell. Truly these excuses are like the rubbish round the walls of Jerusalem in Nehemiah's days. They would all soon disappear if, like the Jews, you had "a mind to work." I say for the last time, Will you not repent and read your Bible?

Believe me, believe me, the *Bible* itself is the best witness of its own inspiration. The men who quibble and make difficulties about inspiration are too often the very men who never read the Scriptures at all. The darkness and hardness and obscurity they profess to complain of are far more often in their own hearts than in the book. Oh, be persuaded! Take it up and begin to read.

2. Is the Bible the Word of God? Then be sure you always *read it with deep reverence.* Say to your soul, whenever you open the Bible, "O my soul, thou art going to read a message from God." The sentences of judges, and the speeches of kings, are received with awe and respect. How much more reverence is due to the words of the Judge of judges

and King of kings! Avoid, as you would cursing and swearing, that irreverent habit of mind into which some modern divines have unhappily fallen, in speaking about the Bible. They handle the contents of the holy book as carelessly and disrespectfully as if the writers were such men as themselves. They make one think of a child composing a book to expose the fancied ignorance of his own father,-or of a pardoned murderer criticising the handwriting and style of his own reprieve. Enter rather into the spirit of Moses on Mount Horeb: "Put thy shoes from off thy feet; the place whereon thou standest is holy ground."

3. Is the Bible the Word of God? Then be sure you never read it without *fervent prayer for the help and teaching of the Holy Spirit.* Here is the rock on which many make shipwreck. They do not ask for wisdom and instruction, and so they find the Bible dark, and carry nothing away from it. You should pray for the Spirit to guide you into all truth. You should beg the Lord Jesus Christ to "open your understanding," as He did that of His disciples. The Lord God, by whose inspiration the book was written, keeps the keys of the book, and alone can enable you to understand it profitably. Nine times over in one Psalm does David cry, "Teach me." Five times over, in the same Psalm, does he say, "Give me understanding." Well says John Owen, Dean of Christ Church, Oxford, "There is a sacred light in the Word: but there is a covering and veil on the eyes of men, so that they cannot behold it aright. Now, the removal of this veil is the peculiar work of the Holy Spirit." Humble prayer will throw more light on your Bible than Poole, or Henry, or Scott, or Burkitt, or Bengel, or Alford, or Wordsworth, or Barnes, or Ellicott, or Lightfoot, or any commentary that ever was written.

The Bible is a large book or a small one, a dark or a bright one, according to the spirit in which men read it. Intellect alone will do nothing with it. Wranglers and first-class men will not understand it unless their hearts are right as well as their heads. The highest critical and grammatical knowledge will find it a sealed book without the teaching of the Holy Ghost. Its contents are often "hid to the wise and prudent and revealed to babes." Remember this, and say always, when you open your Bible, "O God, for Christ's sake, give me the teaching of the Spirit."

4. Finally, is the Bible the Word of God? Then let us all resolve *from this day forward to prize the Bible more.* Let us not fear being idolaters of this blessed book. Men may easily make an idol of the Church, of ministers, of sacraments, or of intellect. Men cannot make an idol of the Word. Let us regard all who would damage the authority of the Bible, or impugn its credit, as spiritual robbers. We are travelling through a wilderness: they rob us of our only guide. We are voyaging over a stormy sea: they rob us of our only compass. We are toiling over a weary road: they pluck our staff out of our hands. And what do these spiritual robbers give us in place of the Bible? What do they offer as a safer guide and better provision for our souls? Nothing! absolutely nothing! Big swelling words! Empty promises of new light! High sounding jargon; but nothing substantial and real! They would fain take from us the bread of life, and they do not give us in its place so much as a stone. Let us turn a deaf ear to them. Let us firmly grasp and prize the Bible more and more, the more it is assaulted.

Let us hear the conclusion of the whole matter; God has given us the Bible to be a light to guide us to everlasting life. Let us not neglect this precious gift. Let us read it diligently, walk in its light, and we shall be saved.

The following quotations about inspiration, from the works of four eminent British theologians, I venture to think deserve attentive perusal. They are valuable in themselves on account of the arguments which they contain.

They also supply abundant proof that the high view of verbal inspiration, which I advocate in this paper, is no modern invention, but an "old path," in which many of God's ablest children have walked, and found it a good way.

1. Bishop Jewell, author of the "Apology," was unquestionably one of the most learned of the English Reformers. Let us hear what he says:-

"St. Paul, speaking of the Word of God, saith, 'the whole Scripture is given by inspiration of God, and is profitable.' Many think the Apostle's speech is hardly true of the whole Scripture,-that all and every part of the Scripture is profitable. Much is spoken of genealogies and pedigrees, of lepers, of sacrificing goats and oxen, etc. These seem to have little profit in them: to be idle and vain. If they show vain in thine eyes, yet hath not the Lord set them down in vain? The words of the Lord are pure words, as the silver tried in a furnace of earth refined seven times. There is no sentence, no clause, no word, no syllable, no letter, but it is written for thy instruction: there is not one jot but it is sealed and signed with the blood of the Lamb. Our imaginations are idle, our thoughts are vain: there is no idleness, no vanity, in the Word of God. Those oxen and goats which were sacrificed teach thee to kill the uncleanness and filthiness of thine heart: they teach thee that thou art guilty of death, when thy life must be redeemed by the death of some beast: they lead thee to believe the forgiveness of sins by a more perfect sacrifice, since it was not possible that the blood of bulls or of goats should take away sins. That leprosy teacheth thee the uncleanness and leprosy of thy soul. These genealogies and pedigrees lead us to the birth of our Saviour Christ, so that the whole Word of God is pure and holy. No word, no letter, no syllable, nor point or tittle thereof, but is written and preserved for thy sake."-*Jewell on the Holy Scriptures.*

2. Richard Hooker, author of the "Ecclesiastical Polity," is justly re-
spected by all schools of thought in the Church of England as the judicious Hooker." Let us hear what he says:-

"Touching the manner how men, by the Spirit of Prophecy in Holy
Scripture, have spoken and written of things to come, we must understand that as the knowledge of that they spake, so likewise *the utterance
of that they knew*, came not by those usual and ordinary means whereby
we are brought to understand the mysteries of our salvation, and are
wont to instruct others in the same. For whatsoever we know, we have
it by the hands and ministry of men, who led us along like children from
a letter to a syllable, from a syllable to a word, from a word to a line,
from a line to a sentence, from a sentence to a side, and so turn over. But
God Himself was their instructor. He Himself taught them, partly by
dreams and visions in the night, partly by revelations in the day, taking
them aside from amongst their brethren, and talking with them as a man
would talk with his neighbours in the way. Thus they became acquainted
even with the secret and hidden counsels of God; they saw things which
themselves were not able to utter, they beheld that whereat men and
angels are astonished, they understood in the beginning what should
come to pass in the last days. God, who lightened thus the eyes of their
understanding, giving them knowledge by unusual and extraordinary
means, *did also miraculously Himself frame and fashion their words
and writings*, insomuch that a greater difference there seemeth not to
be between the manner of their knowledge, than there is between the
manner of their speech and ours. 'We have received,' saith the Apostle,
'not the spirit of the world, but the Spirit which is of God, that we might
know the things that are given to us of God: which things also we speak,
not in words which man's wisdom teacheth, but which the Holy Ghost
doth teach.' This is that which the Prophets mean by those books written

full within and without; which books were so often delivered them to eat, not because God fed them with ink and paper, but to teach us that so often as He employed them in this heavenly work, *they neither spake nor wrote any word of their own, but uttered syllable by syllable as the Spirit put it in their mouths*, no otherwise than the harp or the lute doth give a sound according to the direction of his hands that holdeth it and striketh it with skill."-*Hooker's Works*. Vol. iii. pp. 537, 540.

3. John Owen, Dean of Christ Church, Oxford, was the most learned and argumentative of the Puritans. Let us hear what he says:-

"Holy men of God spake as they were moved by the Holy Ghost. When the word was thus brought to them it was not left to their own understandings, wisdom, minds, memories, to order, dispose, and give it out; but they were borne, actuated, carried out by the Holy Ghost, to speak, deliver, and write all that, and nothing but that,-to very tittles,-that was so brought unto them. They invented not words themselves, suited to the things they had learned, but only expressed the word that they received. Though their mind and understanding were used in the choice of words (whence arise all the differences in their manner of expression), yet they were so guided that their words were not their own, but immediately supplied unto them. Not only the doctrine they taught was the word of truth,-truth itself,-but the words whereby they taught it were words of truth from God Himself. Thus, allowing the contribution of proper instruments for the reception and representation of words which answer to the mind and tongue of the Prophets in the coming of the voice of God to them,-every apex of the written Word is equally divine, and as immediately from God as the voice wherewith, or whereby, He spake to us in the Prophets; and is therefore accompanied with the same authority in itself and to us." -*Owen on the Divine Original of the Scripture*. Vol xvi. p. 305.

4. Dr. Chalmers was probably the most intellectual and deep-thinking theologian that intellectual Scotland has ever produced. Let us hear what he says:

(a) "The subject-matter of the Bible had to pass through the minds of the selected Prophets and Apostles, and to issue thence in language ere it comes forth in the shape of Scripture upon the world. Now it is here that we meet the advocates of a partial or mitigated inspiration, and would make common cause against one and all of them. There is not one theory short, by however so little, of a thorough and perfect inspiration,-there is not one of them but is chargeable with the consequence, that the subject-matter of revelation suffers and is deteriorated in the closing footsteps of its progress; and just before it settles into that ultimate position, where it stands forth to guide and illuminate the world. It existed purely in heaven. It descended purely from heaven to earth. It was deposited purely by the great Agent of revelation in the minds of the Apostles. But then we are told that when but a little way from the final landing place, then, instead of being carried forward purely to the situation where alone the great purpose of the whole movement was to be fulfilled, then was it abandoned to itself, and then were human infirmities permitted to mingle with it, and to mar its lustre. Strange, that just when entering on the functions of an authoritative guide and leader to mankind, that then, and not till then, the soil and the feebleness of humanity should be suffered to gather around it. Strange, that, with the inspiration of thoughts, it should make pure ingress into the minds of the Apostles; but wanting the inspiration of words should not make pure egress to that world in whose behalf alone, and for whose admonition alone, this great movement originated in heaven, and terminated in earth. Strange, more especially strange, in the face of the declaration that not unto themselves but unto us they ministered these things,-strange, nevertheless, that this revelation should come in purely to themselves, but to us should come forth impurely, with somewhat, it would appear, with somewhat the taint and the obscuration of human frailty attached to it.-It matters not at what point in the progress of this celestial truth to our world the obscuration has been cast upon it. It comes to us a dim and desecrated thing at last; and man instead of holding converse with God's unspotted testimony, has an imperfect, a mutilated Bible put into his hands."

(b) "Such being our views, it is the unavoidable consequence of them that we should hold the Bible, for all the purposes of a revelation, to be perfect in its language, as well as perfect in its doctrine. And for this conclusion it is not necessary that we should arbitrate between the theories of superintendence and suggestion. The superintendence that would barely intercept the progress of error, we altogether discard, conceiving, that, if this term be applicable to the process of inspiration at all, it must be that efficient superintendence which not only secures that, negatively, there shall be nothing wrong,-but which also secures that, affirmatively, there should at all times have emanated from the sacred penmen, the fittest topics, and these couched in the fittest and most appropriate expression. Whether this has been affected partly by superintendence and partly by suggestion, or wholly by suggestion, we care not. We have no inclination and no taste for these distinctions. Our cause is independent of them; nor can we fully participate in the fears of those alarmists who think that our cause is materially injured by them. The important question with us is not the process of the manufacture, but the qualities of the resulting commodity. The former we bold not to be a relevant, and we are not sure that it is a legitimate inquiry. It is on the latter we take our stand; and the superabundant testimonies of Scripture on the worth and the perfection and the absolute authority of the Word-these form the strongholds of an argument that goes to establish all which the most rigid advocates for a total and infallible inspiration ought to desire. Our concern is with the work, and not with the workmanship; nor need we intrude into the mysteries of the hidden operation, if only assured by the explicit testimonies of Scripture that the product of that operation, is, both in substance and expression, a perfect directory of faith and practice. We believe that, in the composition of that record, men not only thought as they were inspired, but spake as they were moved by the Holy Ghost. But our argument for the absolute perfection of Holy Writ is invulnerably beyond the reach even of those who have attempted to trace with geographical precision the line which separates the miraculous from the natural; and tell us when it was that Apostles wrote the words which the Spirit prompted them, and when it was that they wrote the words which the Spirit permitted them. To the result, in our humble apprehension, it positively matters not. Did they speak the words that the Spirit prompted,-these words were therefore the best. Did they speak the words which the Spirit permitted,-it was because these words were the best. *The optimism of the Bible is alike secured in both these ways*; and the sanction of the Spirit extended, both in respect of sentiments nod of sayings, to every clause of it. In either way, they effectively are the words of the Spirit; and God through the Bible is not presenting truths through the medium of others' language. He in effect has made it His own language; and God, through the Bible, is speaking to us."

(c) "It is the part of Christians to rise like a wall of fire around the integrity and inspiration of Scripture; and to hold them as intact and inviolable as if a rampart were thrown around them whose foundations are on earth and whose battlements are in heaven. It is this tampering with limits that destroys and defaces everything; and therefore it is pre-cisely when the limit is broken that the alarm should be sounded. If the battle-cry is to be lifted at all, it should be lifted at the outset; and so on the first mingling, by however so slight an infusion, of things human with things divine, all the friends of the Bible should join heart and hand against so foul and fearful a desecration."-*Chalmers' Christian Evidences,* Vol. ii. pp. 371, 372, 375, 376, 396.

FOOTNOTES

1 Carlyle's estimate of the Koran is given, in "Hero-worship," in the following words. "It is a wearisome, confused jumble, crude, recondite, abounding in endless iterations, long-windedness, entanglement, insupportable stupidity. In short nothing but a sense of duty could carry any European through the Koran, with its unreadable masses of lumber."

John Owen says, "There are no other writings in the world, beside the Bible, that ever pretended unto a divine original, but they are not only from their matter, but from the manner of their writing, and the plain footsteps of human artifice and weakness therein, sufficient for their own conviction, and do openly discover their own vain pretensions." (*The Reason of Faith. Works,* vol iv., p. 34, Johnston's Edition.)

2 "I have always been strongly in favour of secular education in the sense of education without theology. But I must confess I have been no less seriously perplexed to know by what practical measures the religious feeling, which is the essential basis of conduct, could be kept up in the present chaotic state of opinion on these matters without the use of the Bible."

"Consider the great historical fact that for three centuries this Book has been woven into the life of all that is best and noblest in English history;-that it has become the national epic of Britain, and is as familiar to noble and simple from John o' Groat's Home to the Land's End, as Dante and Tasso once were to the Italians;-that it is written in the best and purest English, and abounds in exquisite beauties of mere literary form,-and finally, that it forbids the veriest hind who never left his village to be ignorant of other countries and other civilizations, and of a great past, stretching back to the furthest limits of the oldest nations in the world. By the study of what other book could children be so much humanized and made to feel that each figure in that vast historical procession fills, like themselves, but a momentary space in the interval between two eternities, and earns the blessings or the curses of all time, according to its effort to do good and hate evil, even as they also are earning their payment for their work?"-Professor Huxley on School Boards (*Huxley's Critiques and Essays*, p 51.)

3 "The Bible is the fountain of all true patriotism and loyalty in States,-it is the source of all true wisdom, sound policy, and equity in Senates, Council-chambers, and Courts of Justice -it is the spring of all true discipline and obedience, and of all valour and chivalry, in armies and fleets, in the battlefield and on the wide sea;-it is the origin of all probity and integrity in commerce and in trade, in marts and in shops, in banks and exchanges, in the public resorts of men and the secret silence of the heart; it is the pure, unsullied fountain of all love and peace, happiness, quietness and joy, in families and households.-Wherever it is duly obeyed it makes the desert of the world to rejoice and blossom as the rose."-*Wordsworth on Inspiration*, p. 113.

4 "The little ark of Jewish literature still floats above the surges of time, while mere fragments of the wrecked archives of the huge oriental empires, as well as of the lesser kingdoms that surrounded Judea, are now and then cast on our distant shores. "-*Rogers on the Superhuman Origin of the Bible*, p. 311,

5 "We affirm that the Bible is the Worn of God, and that it is not marred with human infirmities. We do not imagine, with some, that the Bible is like a threshing-floor, on which wheat and chaff lie mingled

together, and that it is left for the reader to winnow and sift the wheat from the chaff by the fan and sieve of his own mind."-*Wordsworth on "Inspiration."* (P. 11.)

6 It would be easy to multiply texts in proof of this point. I will only name the following: Heb. ii. 8; iii. 7-19; iv. 2-11; xii. 27.

7 "The language of Scripture is necessarily adapted to the common state of man's intellectual development, in which he is not supposed to be possessed of science. Hence the phrases used by Scripture are precisely those which science soon teaches man to consider inaccurate. Yet they are not on that account the less fitted for their purpose, for if any terms had been used adapted to a more advanced state of knowledge, they must have been unintelligible to those to whom the Scripture was first addressed."-*Whewell's Philosophy of Inductive Science.* Vol. i., p. 636.

www.ingramcontent.com/pod-product-compliance
Lightning Source LLC
Chambersburg PA
CBHW061150120626
46546CB00005B/2000